Everyday Spiritual Warfare

by Amy Barkman

Everyday Spiritual Warfare

© 2011, 2016 by Amy Barkman

All Scripture quotations are from the King James Version.

Barkman, Amy
Everyday Spiritual Warfare

ISBN-13: 978-0-9983520-0-8

About *Everyday Spiritual Warfare*

This is a helpful manual that reminds the Body of Christ of the tremendous responsibility and awesome power we have through the Holy Spirit. Enjoy this book from Amy Barkman and be empowered to step out and up in Faith.

Dr. Stephen Swisher
Senior Pastor
United Methodist Church, Columbus OH

Our everyday world is full of battles with the world, the flesh, and the devil. So we must understand Everyday Spiritual Warfare to live the **victorious** life Jesus died for us to enjoy in the power and authority of His mighty name. Rev. Amy Barkman draws from her depths of wisdom and experience, grounded in the Word of God and Biblical principles of the Kingdom of God, to passionately teach us the weapons of our warfare and the victory we have in Jesus our Lord.

Reverend Tommy Hays
author of *Free to Be Like Jesus*
and Executive Director of Messiah Ministries
www.messiah-ministries.org

Everyday Spiritual Warfare provides much-needed insight into the spiritual struggles that impact our day-to-day lives. Though full of depth and wisdom, the truths explained in this book are easy to understand and applicable to all Christians. I love the list of key scriptures at the end of each chapter. The prayer guide and discussion questions make this book perfect for individuals and groups.

Virginia Smith
bestselling author of *The Days of Noah*
and the Tales from the Goose Creek B&B series
www.virginiasmith.org

In *Everyday Spiritual Warfare* Amy Barkman has equipped us with the gospel armor we need to go forward to battle against the daily challenges of life. In clear and easy to understand prose, she shares the wisdom and joy of the Scripture while encouraging readers to reach for and embrace God's love.

Ann H. Gabhart
bestselling author of *Angel Sister* and the Shaker series
www.annhgabhart.com

Everyday Spiritual Warfare is a practical and useful book for any Christian who seeks to understand and have victory over the warfare we all encounter daily. The author not only explains the principles of spiritual warfare, she then gives us the tools we need to fight specific battles. This book is definitely a must-read.

Tracy Ruckman
Publisher
www.WriteIntegrity.com

Acknowledgements

I owe a huge thank you to my Christian writer's critique group: Virginia Smith, Tracy Ruckman, Amy Smith, Vicki Tiede, Richard Leonard, Sherry Kyle, and Ann Knowles. They gave so many helpful suggestions and I took most of them. If there are glaring errors, they probably tried to get me to change them!

Another huge thank you to the Monthly Manna group who all studied and discussed and some put into practice the concepts of this book. Regular members were Jacque Lea, Carolyn Hawkins, Walter and Renee Knies, Coleen Frisbe, Joanne Clem, Margie Britton, Brian Marlowe, and Lisa Hunter. And thank you to the others who came sometimes and added their wisdom.

I am grateful to my cheering squad, my husband Gary, daughters Ginny Smith, Susie Smith, and Beth Marlowe, and lifelong friend, Jacque Lea. It's wonderful to have people who believe in you when you have a hard time believing in yourself.

I couldn't have received the wisdom from God without my prayer partners: Jacque Lea, Gary Barkman, Joanne Clem, David Moore, Tracy Ruckman, and Ginny Smith.

I am humbled and grateful for those who were willing to endorse this book: Rev. Tommy Hays who has taught me so much about prayer, Anne Gabhart, one of my favorite novelists, Dr. Stephen and Kellie Swisher whom I admire for all their ministries including "Believers Stand United," Virginia Smith, one of my other favorite novelists, and Tracy Ruckman, publisher, author, and friend.

Above all of course I thank and praise my Heavenly Father, Lord Jesus Christ, and Holy Spirit from whom come all wisdom and knowledge.

Right next to God, my gratitude goes to the main one He used to bring this book into existence. You've seen her name four times already - my daughter Virginia (Ginny) Smith. She asked me to write it in the first place, did the critiquing, cheering, and praying mentioned above, and then said, "It's time to get this out there!"

May her faith in the wisdom here be rewarded by much fruit in the lives of the readers.

Amy Barkman

Everyday Spiritual Warfare

Table of Contents

Start From the Beginning!

Dear Reader,

The temptation with this book is to skip forward to the section that interests or troubles you most. But to have it be most effective for you, please begin at the beginning.

The first three chapters outline basic principles of spiritual warfare upon which the rest of the book relies. The fourth chapter gives an overall view of the war we are engaged in. The fifth chapter gives you an important key to all battles against the enemy.

And after that each chapter has information that will help you process the following chapters information more easily.

I believe you are reading this book at this time in your life because God has arranged a divine appointment for you with information that will make you victorious in life and advance the Kingdom of God in the earth.

You may want to use the appendix after reading each chapter for prayer and/or study before you proceed to the next chapter. Or you may want to use these aids at a later time.

Grace, Peace, Blessings, and Freedom be yours in Christ Jesus!

Amy Barkman, September 2011

Everyday Spiritual Warfare

Chapter One

Spiritual Warfare Principles I

Praise the Lord for His mercy endureth forever.
II Chronicles 20:21

I came up out of the baptismal waters with eager anticipation. Rising to newness of life - what a relief. But as soon as I got to the changing room it was obvious that my extra twenty pounds rose with me. And the straight auburn hair I'd longed for all my life had not replaced my curly brown tresses. Within an hour there was no question about the desire to smoke a cigarette passing away; it didn't. By the end of the month the blood test proved that my triglyceride level was still as high as ever. "Hey God, what happened? I thought you said all things would be made new."

There's a story in the Bible that reminds me of the way I felt after my baptism.

The Nation of Judah settled in the land that God promised them. And most of their enemies were destroyed in battle. But one day three armies showed up to surround them.

King Jehoshaphat called a fast and they all went to God in prayer. They said, in essence, "Hey, God, what

3

happened? Here are three armies come to destroy us. They are from the three tribes you wouldn't let us destroy when we came into this land. We don't have any power against them so we're looking to you. You do something!"

One day, many years after my disappointing baptismal experience, I was reading this story and the Holy Spirit whispered to me, "Look up the meaning of the names of those three armies." So I did. The three armies are Moab, Ammon, and Mt. Seir.

Moab means "of the father," Ammon means "tribal," and Mt. Seir means "goat or devil." Light dawned into my mind concerning the plight of the reborn, new creature in Christ that is the true Church.

We who accept Jesus Christ as our savior are born again. We begin a brand new life – the promised land. And just by that act of receiving Jesus as Savior, we defeat more enemies than we can imagine. But there are three enemies that are left in our promised land. Three armies that come against us to destroy.

Moab, "of the father," is symbolic of the genetic conditions we inherit in our bodies and personalities. When we are born again we do not get a new body but are stuck with the DNA given to us.

Ammon, "tribal," is symbolic of the cultural situation into which we are born.

When we are born again, we are not transported into a perfect society but are bombarded all our lives with the evils in the world around us.

Mt. Seir, "goat or devil," is symbolic of the forces of the devil who comes to kill, steal, and destroy. When we are born again, we are not automatically placed out of reach of the enemy.

We are born again children of God with the new life He promised but these three armies want to destroy us. And here they are – right in the promised land – genetic inheritance, cultural surroundings, and the devil with his destructive forces.

You may ask, "Why doesn't God get rid of these enemies for us?" The answer is simple. He will. God did not leave these three enemy armies here so they could destroy us. He says to us, just as He said to His chosen people centuries ago, "... Be not afraid nor dismayed by reason of this great multitude; for the battle is not yours, but God's" (II Chronicles 20:15).

His plan is to overcome them.

Paul wrote "... we are more than conquerors through him that loved us" (Romans 8:37).

What does it mean to be more than a conqueror? The Greek word means preeminently victorious, or a winner before you even enter the battle. Wow! That's good news indeed. And that is what God wants us to understand and practice.

But the way of winning battles through God is not the way of the world. "The weapons of our warfare are not carnal, but mighty through God to the pulling down of strong holds" (II Cor. 10:4). There are some basic principles of spiritual warfare and we have to learn them if we are going to be winners in life. The first, and most important, principle is:

ONLY GOD CAN SUCCESSFULLY DEFEAT EVIL

This doesn't mean there is nothing you can do. God's Instruction Book, the Bible, is full of exhortations such as, "Submit yourselves therefore to God. Resist the devil and he will flee from you" (James 4:7) and "Put on the whole armor of God, that you may be able to stand against the wiles of the devil" (Ephesians 6:11). You are to resist the devil and stand against his schemes.

But did you notice? When your battle against the devil is mentioned, your relationship with God is also mentioned. You can't win against evil in your own strength. But God won't win in this physical realm without your cooperation.

When the nation of Judah sought the Lord for help against the armies that came to destroy them, they were told to present themselves but not to fight. Their response was to put a group of singers in the forefront of the army. Order of presentation was a way of protection in ancient times. The strong men, who were trained and able to fight, were at the forefront when meeting an opposing force, with the women, children, elderly and weak at the rear in the place of protection.

This time, however, the strong fighting men were among those being protected and the singers and praisers, which may have included women and children, went out first. We are told that when they began to sing and to praise God for His mercy, the Lord Himself caused the three armies to be defeated.

This story illustrates several principles of spiritual warfare. The first is evident and stated above ... only God can successfully defeat evil.

"Through God we shall do valiantly: for he it is that shall tread down our enemies" (Psalm 108:13).

The second basic principle of spiritual warfare is:

PRAISING GOD BRINGS HIM ON THE SCENE

This principle is illustrated in the story we just examined. When the tribe of Judah praised God for His mercy to them, He showed no mercy to their enemies but caused them to be destroyed. "And when they began to sing and to praise, the Lord set ambushments against the children of Ammon, Moab, and mount Seir, which were come against Judah; and they were smitten" (II Chronicles 20:22).

King David, from an earlier time in the history of God's people, mentioned this principle in several of his songs. He sang, "I will sing praise to thy name, O thou most High. When mine enemies are turned back, they shall fall and perish at thy presence" (Psalm 9: 2, 3). When David sang praises to the name of God, He showed up in person.

What does it mean to sing praises to the Name of God? In today's society, we have largely lost the understanding of names. When ancient men talked about the name of something or someone, they were talking about its or their essential nature or character.

God revealed Himself to Israel throughout the centuries by His Names through His actions. He revealed Himself, His essential nature, His character, as

Jehovah Jireh – the Lord your Provider
Jehovah Rapha – the Lord your Healer
Jehovah Tsidkenu– the Lord your
   Righteousness
Jehovah Rohi – the Lord your Shepherd
Jehovah Shalom – the Lord your Peace

He revealed other aspects of Himself through names and eventually revealed Himself as Jesus – the Lord your Salvation.

When we praise His name, we are to be praising that aspect of Himself that we need to see active in our situation. Jesus quoted Psalm 8: 2, "Out of the mouth of babes and sucklings has thou ordained strength because of thine enemies, that thou mightest still the enemy and the avenger." He quoted it on the occasion that we know as Palm Sunday when the chief priests and scribes were upset because the children were crying out, "Hosanna to the son of David" (Matthew 21: 15,16).

Hosanna is a word which means "Save." By shouting out that word to Him, the children were recognizing Jesus

7

as the Messiah, the Savior - and the religious people didn't like it. Jesus then quoted Psalm 8, but instead of saying, "out of the mouths of children you have ordained strength", He said, "out of the mouths of children you have ordained praise." Jesus equated strength and praise, validating this principle that your battles are won by God as you praise Him for His mercy toward you in that area.

Some people say "Praise the Lord!" a lot. And there is certainly nothing wrong with saying that, but think about it. If you are going to praise a family member or friend, you don't just say "Praise Richard!" or "Praise Tracy!" You say "Richard has a wonderful sense of humor." Or "Tracy is very generous and kind." So it should be with God. To truly praise Him is to announce gratitude for His specific acts and attributes. And most often it will be as the army of Judah proclaimed, "Praise the Lord for His mercy endures forever."

One problem in our society that keeps us from understanding this principle is our picture of God as separate from us, doling out punishment or reward from outside our world. Many see God as an old man sitting on a throne pointing a finger downward toward earth and shooting lightning bolts to affect the physical realm. We can't praise Him if we don't really understand what He is like.

The apostle John opens his gospel by giving us the true nature of God. "In the beginning was the Word, and the Word was with God, and the Word was God" (John 1:1). God is Spirit, Jesus tells us in John 4:24. He is Person who defines Himself by concepts and ideas. The very meaning of the word Word is "thought expressed." WORD becomes flesh and has ever since God defined and spoke the physical universe into existence with the concept "Light!" Light energy is the basic component for all physical existence. God and His Word are the source of all

8

Life. When we understand that, we can praise Him for being the ongoing Creator.

This concept of God as Spirit and Word is too big for our finite minds to understand completely all at once. But when we plant the seed of understanding and let it grow, we will one day know why Jesus told us that the parable of the sower sowing the Word was necessary for understanding all He teaches (Mark 4:13, 24). God is Spirit and He defines Himself in words. Those spoken words change our circumstances. To praise Him for specific actions and attributes is to bring those actions and attributes into the physical realm. "It is the spirit that quickens; the flesh profits nothing; the words that I speak to you, they are spirit, and they are life" (John 6:63).

We need to recognize that the devil and his followers are also spirit – evil spirits. They convey evil concepts - ideas and concepts that are contrary to the thoughts that God expresses to you through His Word. Just as we know God is not an old man sitting on a throne, the devil is not a man in a red suit holding a pitchfork, and evil spirits are not gargoyles. The Spirit realm, both good and evil, wants to affect the physical realm.

The more we understand God's nature, the more we will praise Him, and the more we praise Him, the more we will see Him active in our lives.

The story of Jehoshaphat and the battle against the three armies illustrates a third principle.

EVIL ATTACKS ON THREE FRONTS

We've already looked at those three fronts in the account described in II Chronicles 20. Remember that in the Bible, names are very important because a name designates the nature of something. We often miss a lot of information that God wants to convey to us in His Word by not discovering what a person or group or place symbolizes.

The first thing I noticed the day the Lord was teaching me from this passage was that the third army is not mentioned at the beginning. "It came to pass after this also that the children of Moab, and the children of Ammon, and **with them other beside** the Ammonites, came against Jehoshaphat to battle" (II Chronicles 20:1).

Moab, representing our genetic inheritance, and Ammon, representing our cultural situation are identified right away. The third army is only mentioned as "and with them, other besides." The group that came along with the first two armies isn't named until verse 10.

"And now, behold, the children of Ammon and Moab and Mount Seir, whom thou would not let Israel invade, when they came out of the land of Egypt ..." Mount Seir comes along with those things that attack us through our birth and cultural situations in life. As we saw earlier, the name Mount Seir means "goat or devil" and represents evil spirits, devils, demons, messengers of the enemy.

Spiritual enemies, evil spirits or devils, cannot just attack you physically – they have no bodies; they come in with the inherited and cultural enemies of your perfect happiness and your perfect good. When something has been established in you through your family heritage or cultural situation, then spiritual evil comes along with it to create and insure a stronghold.

My father's family has a history of blood lipid disorder so out of balance that it was reported in medical journals. My brother and sister and I were the subjects of experimental research to develop drugs to reduce blood lipids. I inherited this disorder as extremely high triglycerides. With medication and moderate obedience to dietary good sense, my triglycerides stay at a healthy level, for me. Without medication and eating right, I get very sick.

The proclivity to high triglycerides is a genetic thing (Moab); the wrong diet is a cultural thing (Ammon); and the enemy (Mount Seir) comes along with those things to kill, steal, and destroy my life and the ministry that the Lord Jesus wants to accomplish through me. But when I praise Him for His mercy and thank Him that He is my life and my health, I receive His health and restoration, even when I have been unwise.

When the people of Judah went to God with their plea for help, they reminded Him that He would not let them invade and destroy these three armies at the time they entered the promised land. He left these possible enemies in the land.

In the same way, when you became a Christian you did not get a new body with a new genetic makeup. You were not translated into a perfect society with perfect cultural habits.

You were left with your genetic and cultural situation in a place where evil spirits operate through these things to kill, steal, and destroy all that God has promised you. In other words, you are in a war against the flesh, the world, and the devil. And you can't win.

But God can.

THINGS TO REMEMBER

> ### Principles of Spiritual Warfare
>
> 1.   Only God can successfully defeat evil.
>
> 2.   Praising God brings Him on the scene.
>
> 3.   Evil attacks on three fronts.

Scripture Truths

"Be not afraid nor dismayed by reason of this great multitude; for the battle is not yours, but God's."   II Chronicles 20:15

"In the beginning was the Word and the Word was with God and the Word was God."   John 1:1

"And when they began to sing and to praise, the Lord sat ambushments against the children of Ammon, Moab, and mount Seir, which were come against Judah; and they were smitten."   II Chronicles 20:22

"Out of the mouths of babes and sucklings has thou ordained strength because of thine enemies, that thou mightest still the enemy and the avenger."   Psalm 8:2

"I will be glad and rejoice in thee: I will sing praise to thy name, O thou most High. When mine enemies are turned back, they shall fall and perish at thy presence."   Psalm 9:2,3

HE SENT HIS WORD AND HEALED THEM AND DELIVERED THEM FROM THEIR DESTRUCTIONS.
Psalm 107: 20

Chapter Two

Spiritual Warfare Principles II

"I can of mine own self do nothing: as I hear, I judge."
John 5: 30

"By your words you shall be justified, and by your words you shall be condemned."
Matthew 12:37

Many years ago, before I took any psychology courses and before God began to work His love nature into my soul with any success, I said something that still shocks me.

A woman of my acquaintance used to call several times a day and whine about how horrible her life was. She often said "I am such a loser. No matter what I do, nothing ever turns out right. I probably should just go ahead and kill myself." In my own defense I have to tell you I didn't believe her threat for a minute; I believed she was far too self-centered and enamored of herself to end her life.

It was my practice to always listen to unhappy people and sympathize with them, making soothing noises and doing anything I could to brighten the corner where they were. But one weekend my sister was coming to visit and since I only saw her every year or two I determined that my time was going to be devoted to her alone. I informed my friends of this, including the whiner/life-threatener. "Don't call me on Saturday. I will be busy. I'll talk to you Sunday evening."

Nevertheless, Saturday at mid-morning as my sister and I were catching up on our relationship and information, the phone rang and in that time before caller id existed, I always answered the phone in case of a family emergency. Guess who? As soon as I said 'Hello' she began. "I am so unhappy. Guess what my husband has done now?" A long description followed. And then - as usual. "Nothing will ever change. Not even God can help me. I think I should just take a gun to my head and pull the trigger."

The response flew out of my mouth without prior thought. "I think you are right. You are so miserable, you would be better off dead. Go ahead and get it over with."

There was a long silence, full of her shock that almost convinced me of electrical waves bombarding my ear drum. The shock was probably going both ways through the phone wires as I stood there in horrific contemplation of my own words.

Condemning words indeed and I quickly repented and am glad to report that over forty years later, the woman is alive and well. But my words were no more deserving of condemnation, and far less powerfully destructive to her life, than her own words.

In the first chapter on the principles of spiritual warfare, we saw that only God can successfully defeat evil and we saw how He does it - through words spoken from our mouths, through His nature released into the physical atmosphere by our spoken agreement with Him.

We also saw that evil comes to us through our genetic and cultural situations and that the devil and his army come along with those fallen circumstances.

Now we are going to look at another very important principle, a principle that your enemy the devil wants you to never, ever find out about.

The fourth principle of spiritual warfare is:

WHAT YOU BELIEVE AND SPEAK ABOUT GOD'S CHARACTER AND WILL DETERMINES WHAT HE CAN DO FOR YOU

What? Is God not sovereign?

The American Heritage Dictionary defines "sovereign" as "supremacy of authority" and yes, God is the supreme authority in the universe He created. Because that is true, the devil wants us to think that everything that happens is God's will.

But the Bible tells us that from the beginning God turned over His authority in the earth to mankind. "And God said, Let us make man in our image, after our likeness; and let them have dominion..." (Genesis 1:26). And then God rested from His work (Genesis 2:2).

God's work was creating and He created everything by speaking.

"And **God said** 'Let there be light...' **and there was** light" (Genesis 1:3).

"And **God said** 'Let there be a firmament'...**and God made**..." (Genesis 1:6,7).

"And **God said** 'Let the waters... be gathered...' **and it was so**" (Genesis 1:9).

"And **God said** 'Let the earth bring forth'... **and it was so**" (Genesis 1:11).

"And **God said** 'Let there be lights ....' **and it was so**" (Genesis 1:14,15).

"And **God said** 'Let the waters bring forth...' **and God saw**" (Genesis 1:20,21).

"And **God said** 'Let the earth bring forth…' **and it was so**" (Genesis 1:24).

He created everything by speaking it into existence. Then He turned the physical realm over to man for the ongoing work of keeping that realm connected to God through His Word, His authority, in and through them. God has invested His sovereignty in His Word which is received and poured out through the souls and mouths of His people.

When mankind fell away from oneness with God, He said 'the ground is cursed for your sake' (Genesis 3:17). He was <u>not</u> saying, "Because you disobeyed I am going to curse the ground." He <u>was</u> saying "Because you did not choose to stay in harmony with Me, the very earth will suffer."

Paul confirms this in Romans 8 when he writes "For the earnest expectation of creation waits for the manifestation of the sons of God" (verse 19). The physical creation is waiting for us to be in harmony with God and resume our intended role in the earth.

This is so far beyond what we have understood about the way things are that it shakes the foundations of our worldviews. We don't want that kind of responsibility. It is easier to blame the will of God for bad things that happen in the earth. We say "God must have caused or allowed this for a reason."

We don't want to take the responsibility for bringing good things into the earth either. We'd rather sit back and say "If God wants me to have it, He will give it to me." But, over and over in the Bible we are told to exercise faith and change our circumstances.

Faith is defined by the writer of Hebrews in Chapter 11 as "the substance of things hoped for, the evidence of things not seen" (verse 1).

FAITH IS BELIEF THAT SOMETHING YOU WANT BUT CAN'T YET SEE IN THE PHYSICAL REALM IS ACTUALLY TRUE IN THE SPIRITUAL REALM AND WILL EVENTUALLY COME TO PASS IN THE PHYSICAL REALM.

Faith believes that the thing hoped for is a spiritual truth that will come to pass, a word from God that will be made flesh.

And it is faith, the belief that it will happen, which actually is the substance that causes it to happen.

The writer goes on to say in verse 6 of that same chapter, "But without faith it is impossible to please Him; for he that comes to God must believe that He is, and that He is a rewarder of them that diligently seek him."

Faith, the thing that causes what you want to actually happen, is based on your belief that God really is alive and that **He wants good things for you.**

In Romans 10:17, we are told that, "faith comes by hearing and hearing by the word of God." And in II Peter 1:4, we see, "Whereby are given unto us exceeding great and precious promises, that by these you might **be partakers of the divine nature."**

A Word is "a thought expressed." If it is only a thought that has not been expressed, it is not a word. God pours out Words, His expressed thoughts, His concepts, His ideas, His pictures of good things He wants to do for us and through us. If we believe and express by word or deed that those things are His will for us, He is able to bring them to pass.

We live in a world where the father of lies (John 8:44) wants us to believe that bad things are God's will for us. He, the one who hates us and hates God, wants us to believe that his own will for us is God's will for us. The example I gave at the end of the first chapter is a good illustration.

If I believed the devil about God's will for me, I would say, "God allowed" my faulty blood lipid system for a reason and that His plan must be for me to die young (as I almost did at age 23 and again at age 54). He would probably also convince me that my lack of dietary discipline makes me deserve to die young. But the truth is that I was born into a fallen world with genetic evil that I inherited. I am not yet perfected and have faults, including wrong eating habits tied in with emotional insecurities. However, the mercy of the Father and the life given by Jesus to purchase me, soul and body, has overcome the accuser and destroyer's desire to eradicate me from usefulness in the harvest field of God...because I know the devil is a liar and God's Word is true.

The Psalmist wrote in Psalm 103, "Bless the Lord, O my soul, and forget not all His benefits; who forgives all your iniquities, who heals all your diseases; who redeems your life from destruction; who crowns you with lovingkindness and tender mercies; who satisfies your mouth with good things so that your youth is renewed as the eagles" (verses 2 – 5). Why would the Psalmist need to tell himself not to forget the benefits of God? The same reason you need to tell yourself not to forget His benefits. We get so caught up in our connection with the physical world that we forget what God wants to do for us, and often we don't know what He wants to do.

If you believe that God will not forgive some of your sins, or heal some of your diseases, or redeem your life from some destruction, if you believe that He desires to punish instead of give you mercy, if you believe that He wants you to experience hardship and lack, then you will not be able to receive from Him all the good things that He desires to give you.

If you believe He wants bad things to happen to you, you will either receive bad things and assume they come from Him or you will feel that you need to work very hard yourself and fight for the good things in life. And on some level, you will believe that you are fighting against God for the good things.

Jesus said, "Have faith in God. For truly I say to you that whosoever shall say...and shall not doubt in his heart, but shall believe that those things which he says shall come to pass; he shall have whatsoever he says. Therefore (or because this is true) I say to you, what things soever you desire, when you pray believe that you receive them, and you shall have them" (Mark 11:22 – 24).

That is a pretty big statement. Jesus was saying that what you believe in your heart and speak with your mouth will come to pass. He says that because this is true, you are to ask God for whatever you want and believe He gives it to you. Then the good thing you believe will come out your mouth and you will have it.

One of the great keys to getting what you want is to believe that God wants you to have it. This statement from Jesus is not the only time that God promises that whatever you want, He will give to you.

"He that spared not his own Son, but delivered him up for us all, how shall he not with him also freely give us all things"(Romans 8:32)?

"Truly, truly I say to you, whatsoever you shall ask the Father in my name, He will give you" (John 16:23).

The promises that God will give you whatever you want are contingent on only two things:
   (1) Identification with Jesus Christ
   (2) Belief in God's good will toward you.

Unfortunately, most of us, even those who are Christians and should know better, have not been taught to believe in God's good will toward us. We have been given a picture of God that is demanding and legalistic. That image is a lie painted by the "god of this world" (II

Cor. 4:4), the deceiver, the adversary who began painting wrong pictures of God in the garden. His lies about the nature of God were believed then and they are believed now. Because the first humans believed a lie about the nature of God, they missed out on living in Paradise forever. And because you believe lies about the nature of God, you miss out on the wonderful life He wants to give you. The worst sin we commit is attributing to God the destructive will of the devil toward us.

The other problem is that we are not solid in our identification with Jesus Christ.

We may have accepted Him as Savior but we are still not identifying with Him and seeing ourselves as members of His Body in the earth, vessels of the anointed Word.

We Christians tend to see ourselves in different ways. Some people see themselves as being saved in the sense of going to heaven when they die but being continually disciplined by God here and now for their own good. Others see themselves as going to heaven when they die but completely dependent on their own wits and energy for their quality of life on earth. Some see the sacrifice of Jesus merely as something that gave them a chance to earn their way to heaven.

Very few Christians see themselves walking completely in the grace and mercy of God, a vehicle for His character and will in the earth. For this reason very few of us are completely at peace with God. Therefore we may say the words "in His Name" but don't really believe God hears us as if Jesus Himself were making the request.

Until we have a revelation of His complete grace and mercy toward us, we will not receive all the benefits that He desires to give us. Nor can we be the blessing to others that He desires to make us.

The devil knows how God works in the earth. The devil knows that God has placed His sovereignty in His Word.

God is not arbitrary, acting on whims. And He does not prefer any person above another. His Word is given to all human beings, no matter what they have done or not done. And His Word says that "whosoever" believes Him and His promises, and speaks out that agreement with Him, will be blessed.

We don't like to think about ourselves as hindering God's will from coming to pass and yet Jesus said, "I can do nothing by myself; as I HEAR, I judge"(John 5:30). Jesus acts on the Word of God. While we are begging Him to do something, He is waiting for us to speak out the Word of God that causes His will to come to pass in the earth. The Psalmist wrote that the angels hearken to the voice of God's Word (Psalm 103:20). The realm of the Spirit is waiting on you to pour forth God's living concepts from your mouth.

When will we realize that God and His Word are one, and He ordained that His Word in our mouths is the most powerful force in the universe (John 1:1; 7:38)?

The devil realizes it and that is why he works so hard planting his own concepts and ideas in our minds and hearts so that we will speak them out instead.

He wants to bring his will to pass but he can't do it by himself. He has no authority or body by which to speak in the physical realm. He has to steal your authority and get you to release his words, his concepts, ideas, and pictures, into the earth.

You have an enemy who is out to convince you that God is causing bad things to happen to you and others because of sin. He especially wants Christians, "the anointed ones" to believe this so that they will not exercise God's Word to overcome those bad things.

Whether we like it or not, our belief or unbelief in what God promises is the deciding factor on whether His will comes to pass in our lives. We don't realize that much of what we believe and say about God is blasphemy.

Jesus cast out devils and was accused of being empowered by the prince of devils; He called that accusation blasphemy (Matthew 12:31). Isaiah says "Woe unto them that call evil good, and good evil" (Isaiah 5:20). But it happens all the time. God is accused of working evil – causing accidents and sickness. And the devil is sometimes given credit for good things in life – prosperity or success or some of the gifts that the Holy Spirit gives.

Much of what we attribute to God, we have laws against. We would incarcerate a father who purposely broke his children's legs, caused them to have accidents, made them sick, or withheld necessities. Why do we accuse God of these things? God is not a child abuser. He disciplines with His Word. "All scripture is given by inspiration of God and is profitable for doctrine, for reproof, for correction, for instruction in righteousness" (II Timothy 3:16).

The bad things we have attributed to His correction are either the result of our ignorance of His nature and promises, or the result of our walking away from His grace. He doesn't cause the bad things to happen but He does warn us about the bad things to which we expose ourselves when we run from His guidance.

The devil lies to us about the nature of God. We believe those lies, accept evil and call it good. Some of us even preach it from our pulpits instead of preaching the good news of His forgiveness, mercy, and grace. May God forgive us.

If you have ever done that, if you have ever called evil good, blaming bad things on God, and if the Holy Spirit is speaking to you right now to recognize it and repent, please do so and give God permission to "transform you by the renewing of your mind" (Romans 12:2). We are to be transformed into loving, trusting sons of God walking in victory in the earth .

We are told that Jesus "must reign, till he has put all enemies under his feet" (I Cor. 15:25) and it is through His Body, the Church, that He will destroy those enemies (Ephesians 1:17 – 23).

The Psalmist says that God will satisfy your mouth with good things so that your youth is renewed. When you put His Words in your mouth because you believe them in your heart, you will experience all God intended mankind to experience in the days of youth, or as humans were created in the beginning in Paradise.

Isaiah wrote that God said, "Therefore my people are gone into captivity because they have no knowledge; and their honorable men are famished, and their multitude dried up with thirst. Therefore hell has enlarged herself and opened her mouth without measure..." (Isaiah 5:13,14).

Because we have not put God's Word in our mouths as our food and drink, because we have not renewed our minds with His Word, we are taken captive to every evil thing the devil wants to get us to accept in life, and through our words hell enlarges herself because of our lack of knowledge of the goodness of God.

We experience hell on earth because we are not in complete harmony with God.

That's a heavy statement. But it is truth.

If you believe that God is angry with you, you bring into your circumstances the concepts that the "accuser of the brethren" (Revelation 12:10,11) gives you of what God wants you to have in life. If you believe that God's mercy endures forever and that He loves you unconditionally, you will bring His grace into your every circumstance.

John wrote, "If our heart does not condemn us, then we have confidence toward God. And whatsoever we ask, we receive of Him…" (I John 3:21,22).

God is not our problem. One problem is that our hearts and minds are deceived about the nature of God and His will, and the thoroughness of our redemption. The other problem is that our mouths agree with the enemy's concepts instead of God's Word.

"The weapons of our warfare are not carnal but mighty through God to the pulling down of strongholds, casting down imaginations and every high things that exalts itself against the knowledge of God, and bringing into captivity every thought to the obedience of Christ" (II Corinthians 10:4,5).

You are called to cast down from your mind and heart every thought that is contrary to God's grace and love for you through Christ Jesus. You are to believe that His promises are true and that "whatever you ask the Father in my name, He will give it to you" (John 16:23).

Your part is to ask Him for the good things He has promised you in every area of life, trust that His Word is true and He will bring it to pass, and speak out that what you have asked for is yours.

Jesus said, "Out of the abundance of the heart the mouth speaks. A good man out of the good treasure of the heart brings forth good things: and an evil man out of the evil treasure brings forth evil things" (Matthew 12: 34,35).

This is not just a New Testament, Christian truth; it is a truth about mankind in the earth from the beginning. "Death and life are in the power of the tongue" (Proverbs 18:21).

What you believe in your heart and speak with your mouth will come to pass because you are made in the image of God and given authority in the earth.

The writer of Proverbs quotes God as saying "…attend to my words…keep them in the middle of your heart...keep your heart with all diligence for out of it are the issues of life" (Proverbs 4:20-23). We are to protect our hearts from concepts that are not from God and we are to keep any words that disagree with His words out of our mouths.

I know a lady who says over and over "There is a black cloud over our family." She believes that this black cloud is just part of the family lot in life as given by God. That black cloud includes being slighted by service providers, sickness, loss, and many other inconveniences, expenses, and discomforts. Whenever one of these things happens, she says, "It's the black cloud."

Another family member is a believer in God's promises and doesn't buy the black cloud idea for a minute but believes for and receives God's favor in business and other aspects of life. When she asked me to agree with her in prayer about getting rid of the black cloud's effects on that lady, I started to agree and then stopped.

"She will have to agree that it's gone," I said.

"What do you mean?" the family member asked.

I answered, "The black cloud is only alive in her perception of truth. It has no reality without her belief in it. It is her perception that prevents her from receiving all God wants to give her."

We agreed to pray that God change her mistaken perception that both good and evil come from His hand. When she receives that difference of perception, that renewing of her mind, she will not just stop receiving bad things as coming from the hand of God but will begin expecting good things. The "black cloud" will no longer receive empowerment and life from her belief and words. We've already begun to see a difference.

The same thing was true of the woman I spoke about at the beginning of this chapter. When she stopped whining and started believing and expecting God's promises, that allowed Him to give her hope and a future, her life changed for the better.

Believing God's Word in your heart and speaking those concepts with your mouth is your appointed role in the earth as God's representative. It is in this way that the will of God is accomplished "on earth as it is in heaven" (Matthew 6:10).

THINGS TO REMEMBER

Principles of Spiritual Warfare

1. Only God can successfully defeat evil.

2. Praise of God brings God on the scene.

3. Evil attacks on three fronts.

4. What you believe and speak about God's character and will determines what He can do for you.

Scripture Truths

"And Jesus answering said to them, Whosoever shall say...and shall not doubt in his heart but shall believe that those things which he says shall come to pass, he shall have whatsoever he says." Mark 11:22,23

"My son attend to my words; incline your ear to my sayings. Let them not depart from your eyes; keep them in the midst of your heart. For they are life unto those that find them, and health to all their flesh. Keep your heart with all diligence; for out of it are the issues of life. Put away from yourself a froward mouth, and perverse lips put far from you." Proverbs 4:20 - 24

"Death and life are in the power of the tongue." Proverbs 18:21

IF ANY MAN OFFEND NOT IN WORD, THE SAME IS A PERFECT MAN, AND ABLE ALSO TO BRIDLE THE WHOLE BODY....THE TONGUE IS A FIRE...AND SETS ON FIRE THE COURSE OF NATURE; AND IT IS SET ON FIRE BY HELL.

James 3:2,6

Chapter Three

Spiritual Warfare Principles III

"Christ has redeemed us from the curse of the law, being made a curse for us...that the blessing of Abraham might come on the Gentiles through Jesus Christ..."
Galatians 3:13,14

"I knew God wanted me to be a preacher but I wanted to go on working in the mines. One day I fell down a shaft and broke my leg and knew that God finally got me where he wanted me, so I surrendered to the ministry."

When I heard this statement from a fellow student I restrained myself from standing up, pointing my finger, and shouting "Blasphemy!!! Woe unto those who call good evil and evil good." It was hard to keep quiet. I'm still not sure I shouldn't have said something – not that dramatically of course, but something.

Isn't it amazing that we arrest and jail earthly fathers for doing the same things we blame on our heavenly Father? There is nothing that causes me more grief than hearing our Father who is Love, Light, and Life credited with the work of the enemy who is hatred, darkness, and death. God doesn't cause accidents, give diseases, steal money, or cause rejection. There is an enemy in the world and he hates mankind.

I thank God that my fellow student reached out to God during that time but I hope he eventually discovered that God was not the cause of his fall and his broken leg. When we run away from God, we run from His grace and protection. And there is an enemy waiting for us.

At one time in my own life I ran from God's will and ended up in a mess. I took a job that I knew was not God's will for me, because I thought I needed the money. Then I was stuck in the job because I became dependent on the paycheck. I hated the job and experienced lots of stress and many problems before I finally got back on His path for me and learned to trust him for my financial needs. But the mess wasn't God's punishment; it was the natural result of my own disobedience and turning from the One who always protects and provides.

Another principle that your enemy, the devil, does not want you to discover is

GOD ONLY WANTS GOOD THINGS FOR YOU

By this statement, I am not saying that God wants things for you that will feel bad but that are for your own good. I am saying that your delight is His goal.

There is an interesting verse in Psalm 37, "Delight yourself also in the Lord; and He shall give you the desires of your heart" (verse 4). The verse promises that if you delight yourself in Him, you will receive the desires of your heart, not the desires of His heart. However, I have learned that the desires of His heart for me are experienced by me as desires in my own heart. When I am delighting in Him, I desire the things that He desires for me. He loves to delight in my delight.

This concept of God often seems too good to be true. But God is the truest good there is. If it seems to us that He is too good to be true, it is just an indication of the fallen state of our minds, the pollution of our souls by the fruit of the tree of knowledge of good and evil.

James wrote "Do not err, my beloved brethren. Every good gift and every perfect gift is from above, and comes down from the Father of lights..." (James 1:16,17).

In Psalm 112, the writer talks about the will of the enemy and states that for the one whose heart is fixed and trusting in the Lord, "the desire of the wicked shall perish" (verse 10).

The wicked one wants to create strongholds that will insure the perpetuation of your fallen circumstances. The strongholds he creates are in your mind and heart. Stop and think about that. The enemy wants your fallen circumstances to continue. That is why he engineered the fall in the first place. He does not want God's children to experience the fullness of God's love.

Your mind is a battleground. It is the place in this world where the will of God and the will of the devil war. Your will is the deciding factor in the battle; you choose which concept will be made flesh, whose idea will come to pass in your life.

Jesus said, "The thief comes not but for to steal, and to kill, and to destroy. I am come that they might have life, and that they might have it more abundantly" (John 10:10).

Do you believe that?

Do you honestly believe that if something steals, kills, or destroys, it is from the thief and not from God?

Until you settle that question once and for all time, it is very difficult for you to receive from the Giver of all good things, almost impossible.

One scripture verse that is often paraphrased incorrectly is II Corinthians 12:7 "...there was given to me a thorn in the flesh, the messenger of Satan to buffet me, lest I should be exalted above measure. For this thing I besought the Lord thrice, that it might depart from me.

And he said to me 'My grace is sufficient for thee: for my strength is made perfect in weakness."

People often say, "God gave Paul a thorn in the flesh." But the verse clearly says that the thorn in his flesh was a messenger from the devil, not from God. He asked God to make it go away and God said that His power within Paul was sufficient for all Paul needed to be victorious over the enemy. Paul was not like Job who blamed God for the calamities in his life. Of course Job realized his mistake too when He had a revelation of God's person. Paul already had that revelation and as a result was able to see clearly where the persecution was coming from. And when he realized that God's grace was sufficient for him to overcome the persecution and receive favor, he ended up "the aged Paul" in his own house instead of in prison (Philemon 9, Acts 28:30).

The apostle Paul also wrote that "Christ has redeemed us from the curse of the law, being made a curse for us...that the blessing of Abraham might come on the Gentiles through Christ Jesus" (Galatians 3:13,14).

The spiritual warfare principle we learn from that is

CHRISTIANS ARE REDEEMED FROM THE BAD THINGS THAT HAPPEN AS A RESULT OF NOT OBEYING GOD'S LAW

What? Don't we reap what we sow? Isn't it true that what goes around comes around? Yes, unless you are redeemed from that cycle.

The blessings of following God's Law and the curses of disobeying God's Law are outlined in Deuteronomy 28. They cover everything from sickness to success to family relationships to holiness.

In verses 1 and 2, we are told that if we listen to God and do everything He says, the blessings listed will come upon us and overtake us. In verse 15 we are told that if we don't listen to God and do everything He says, the curses that are listed will come upon us and overtake us.

Uh, oh! I don't always listen and do everything God says. So I certainly don't deserve these blessings.

"Blessed in the city and blessed in the field, the fruit of your body blessed, and the fruit of your ground, and the fruit of your cattle, the increase of your kine and the flocks of your sheep. Blessed when you come in and blessed when you go out. The Lord shall cause your enemies that rise up against you to be smitten before your face; they shall come out against you one way, and flee before you seven ways. The Lord shall command the blessing upon you in your storehouses, and in all that you set your hand to, and He shall bless you in the land which the Lord your God has given you. The Lord shall establish you a holy people unto Himself, as He has sworn to you. And all the people of the earth shall see that you are called by the name of the Lord and they shall be afraid of you. And the Lord shall make you plenteous in goods, in the fruit of your body, and in the fruit of your cattle, and in the fruit of your ground, in the land which the Lord swore to your fathers to give you. The Lord shall open to you His good treasure, the heaven to give the rain to your land in His season, and to bless all the work of your hand; and you shall lend to many nations and you shall not borrow. And the Lord shall make you the head and not the tail and you shall be above only and you shall not be beneath. And you shall not go aside from any of the words which I command you this day, to the right hand or to the left, to go after other gods to serve them" (Deuteronomy 28:3 – 14).

Did you see that one of the blessings is that your enemies will be smitten before your face? That was a promise of God to His people for their obedience. We saw in the first chapter that the tribe of Judah went to God and sought His help against their enemies. God fighting for them and destroying their enemies was not just something He did unexpectedly that one time. It was based on a promise to those who listen to and obey God. We have a promise that our enemies will be smitten before our faces. Our enemies are sickness, poverty, confusion, destructive habits, unhappy relationships, failure, and depression.

And yet, we don't listen to and obey all God says for us to do. So that leaves us with the curse, and our enemies in triumph in our lives.

Doesn't it?

Not according to God's promise in Christ Jesus as revealed by the apostle Paul. "Christ has redeemed us from the curse of the law, (being made a curse for us for it is written, 'cursed is everyone that hangs on a tree) so that the blessing of Abraham might come on the Gentiles through Jesus Christ; that we might receive the promise of the Spirit through faith" (Galatians 3:13,14).

According to God, if you are in Christ Jesus, you are redeemed from the curses that come from disobedience. Jesus has borne the curses for you. Wow! Who's been hiding that secret?

God knew that fallen mankind was incapable of listening to and obeying everything He commanded. If we had been capable, we would have no need of a Savior.

Jesus came and died in our place, taking all the curses due us for disobedience. He didn't do this apart from God but as the fulfillment of the heart of God who desires mercy over judgment toward mankind whom He created in His image (James 2:13). "God was in Christ, reconciling the world to himself, not imputing their trespasses to them" (II Corinthians 5:19).

Do you have the spiritual audacity to believe that? Can you believe that no matter what you have done, thought, spoken, or desired wrongly, God is not holding it against you? Can you believe that the blood of Jesus poured out for your sins is actually sufficient to make you acceptable to the Father who is all Holiness?

"He has made us accepted in the beloved, in whom we have redemption through his blood, the forgiveness of sins according to the riches of his grace wherein He has abounded toward us" (Ephesians 1:6-8).

Can you believe it?

And can you believe that redemption is not just for the next life but for this life? One of the most quoted passages of scripture is Psalm 23. The psalmist wrote "Thou preparest a table before me in the presence of mine enemies"(verse 5). You will have no enemies in heaven. That table is for here and now, a gracious feast of blessings laid out for those who trust in the goodness of God and the triumph of His mercy over His judgment toward them, accomplished through the redemptive act of Jesus Christ on the cross at Calvary.

Do you believe it?

It is the desire of the heart of your heavenly Father that you do.

The curses of the law, the consequences of disobedience from which you are redeemed are not listed here. You can read them in their entirety in the book of Deuteronomy, chapter 28, beginning with verse 15.

The rest of this book is concerned with those curses and how to overcome them with the Word of God. The seventh principle of spiritual warfare is like the first one. It is:

YOUR ARMOUR AND WEAPONRY ARE THE WORD OF GOD

The apostle Paul wrote, "Be strong in the Lord and in the power of His might. Put on the whole armor of God, that you may be able to stand against the wiles of the devil, for we wrestle not against flesh and blood, but against principalities, against powers, against the rulers of the darkness of this world, against spiritual wickedness in high places. Wherefore take unto you the whole armour of God..." (Ephesians 6:11-13).

Then after telling us that the armor of God is what will cause us to be able to stand against the schemes of the devil, he lists what that armor is and, as we will see, every bit of the armor has to do with God's Word.

"Stand therefore with your loins girt about with the **truth**" (Ephesians 6:14). The word loins in the original Greek means "seat of generative power". This piece of armor has to do with the power of life and death that is the seat of your creative power. And spiritually the power of life and death is in your mouth. You are to put the truth in your mouth - and His Word is truth (John 17:17). What you believe in your heart and speak will come to pass. So even if you don't yet completely believe all the good news in your heart, put the truth in your mouth anyway. I read once that the psychological makeup of mankind is that he believes what he hears himself say more than what he hears others say.

"and having on the breastplate of **righteousness**..." (Ephesians 6:14). Our heart, our emotional realm, is to be protected by knowing that God loves us just as we are and that our right standing with Him is because of Jesus' sacrifice, not because of our own actions. The breastplate was a two-part protection of the heart, front and back.

According to First Thessalonians 5:8, that breastplate is made up of faith and love. Faith comes by hearing, and hearing by the Word of God, so half of that protection of the heart is belief in God's Word; the other half is to walk in God's love as extended to you through Calvary.

"and your feet shod with the gospel of **peace**..." (Eph. 6:15). The gospel is the Good News – the Word of reconciliation, the power of God to save (I Cor. 1:18). We are to walk in God's peace, no longer at war with Him or estranged from Him, recognizing that "whosoever will" among humans are redeemed from the eternal consequences and the power of sin by the blood of Jesus.

"Above all taking the shield of **faith**..." (Eph. 6: 16). Faith is trusting that God's nature is good and His Word is true. That trust shields us from the lies of the enemy that would have us think God wants bad things to happen to us and that His promises are not for us today.

"And take the helmet of **salvation**..." (Eph. 6:17). We are to be transformed by the renewing of our minds by the Word of God so that the Word of God protects and guards our minds at all times and repels every thought that comes against His promises. We can't believe and bring to pass what we don't know about. We can only know by pouring the truth into these minds. We put on our helmet by reading and studying the Word of our salvation.

"and the sword of the Spirit, which is the **Word** of God" (Eph. 6:17). The Sword of the Spirit is clearly designated the Word of God. Your only weapon against the enemies of life, love, joy, and peace is God's Word which is His spiritual power sent forth to accomplish His will. The only weapon you can successfully use against the evil in this world is the Sword of the Spirit – the word of God. And you use it by hiding it in your heart and speaking it with your mouth. During Jesus' temptation in the wilderness, he always answered the devil with "It is written."

Every piece of this armor has to do with God who is one with His Word. As the Psalmist wrote "I will say of the Lord, He is my refuge and my fortress, my God, in Him will I trust" (Psalm 91:2). We have no refuge other than the Word of God. He and His Word are One.

We live in a world that fell away from oneness with God and we have an enemy who wants things to stay that way. But God has promised victory.

Kay is a Christian who got very distracted from God's will during her high school years. She ended up having a child outside of marriage and receiving no emotional or financial support from the father of the child. Many young women would have said "I deserve this because of my sin," and resigned themselves to a mediocre life. But Kay had been raised knowing that she was redeemed from the curse, knowing that God's mercy was greater than her sinfulness, knowing that God wanted only good things for her life. She went to the Lord, acknowledged her sin, thanked Him for His redemption and for her child, and went on with life. She graduated from college and refused to take a job that was less than the position she believed God had for her. She is now in a job she loves, with a daughter who is a great joy to her.

Kay lives the redeemed life, expecting and receiving good things from God, not because of her actions but because of Jesus' actions and her faith in God's love and mercy and desire to bless her. "Now thanks be to God who always causes us to triumph in Christ"(II Cor. 2:14). "...this is the victory that overcomes the world, our faith" (I John 5:4). "...in all these things we are more than conquerors through Him that loved us" (Romans 8:37).

As we look at the various battles we are confronted with in life, all will be considered in the light of the seven principles of spiritual warfare that we have looked at in the first three chapters.

THINGS TO REMEMBER

Principles of Spiritual Warfare

1. Only God can successfully defeat evil.

2. Praise of God bring God on the scene.

3. Evil attacks on three fronts.

4. What you believe and speak about God's character and will determines what He can do for you.

5. God only wants good things for you.

6. Christians are redeemed from the bad things that happen as a result of not obeying God's law.

7. Your armor and weaponry are the Word of God.

Scripture Truths

"Christ has redeemed us from the curse of the law... so that the blessing of Abraham might come on the Gentiles through Jesus Christ; that we might receive the promise of the Spirit through faith."   Galatians 3:13,14

"The thief comes not but for to steal, and to kill, and to destroy. I am come that they might have life, and that they might have it more abundantly."   John 10:10

" He has made us accepted in the beloved, in whom we have redemption through his blood.."   Ephesians 1:6

"..in all these things we are more than conquerors through Him that loved us." Romans 8:37

FEAR NOT, LITTLE FLOCK; FOR IT IS YOUR FATHER'S GOOD PLEASURE TO GIVE YOU THE KINGDOM. Luke 12:32

Chapter Four

The War Against Chaos

"And the very God of peace sanctify you wholly; and I pray
God your whole spirit and soul and body be preserved
blameless unto the coming of our Lord Jesus Christ."
I Thessalonians 5:23

Before we look at the individual battles that make up
our lives in this world, I want us to see a clear picture of
the war of which those battles are a part. The war is
against chaos. The American Heritage Dictionary defines
"chaos" as "A condition or place of total disorder or
confusion." This state of disorder is against the nature of
the God of Peace.

The word we translate "Peace" from the original
Hebrew is "Shalom" and in the Greek "Eirene." This
word, used to describe God's intention for the earth and
everything in it, means "wholeness, interconnectedness,
completeness" and is sometimes translated health, well-
being, and prosperity because those states indicate the
presence of peace. Anything not complete, whole, or
connected with God may be said to be in some degree of
chaos.

When God created this earth, He created it in a state of
Shalom, perfect connectedness with Himself. Everything

41

was good. His counterpart in the earth, humans made in His image and designed to carry out His will in the physical realm, were completely connected to Him in will, mind, and emotion. His life flowed through them and all was well.

When mankind chose to disconnect, to allow pollution to join their wills, minds, and emotions so that they sometimes brought forth good and sometimes brought forth evil, all creation suffered from that choice. The earth itself began to bring forth both good things and bad. A state of chaos ensued. The physical realm was disconnected from God's perfect plan, no longer whole and complete.

We who live in that fallen state and have so lived in the memory of mankind cannot even picture a world that is totally free from chaos. Indeed, the state of our fallen-ness is so thorough that the concept of perfection often seems boring to us. Most of our greatest excitement in this present state comes from the joy of defeating chaos in the best way we can see to do it. Even the sins we commit are attempts, although using wrong methods, to overcome some evil – lack, loneliness, fear, need, unhappiness. It is hard for us to imagine a continuous joy that is not a triumph over some problem, but just a state of being.

Because we live in a world that is disconnected from God, we can't understand how the world is supposed to work. "My thoughts are not your thoughts, neither are your ways my ways, says the Lord" (Isaiah 55:8). The Lord tells us what His thoughts are in Jeremiah 29:13 "For I know the thoughts that I think toward you, says the Lord, thoughts of peace, and not of evil..." God's thoughts, His concepts of us, are pictures of interconnectedness, wholeness, and completeness; they include health, well-being, and prosperity.

In the beginning, God told mankind that if they ate of the fruit of the tree of knowledge of good and evil, they would die. " for in the day that you eat of it you shall surely die" (Genesis 2:17). My Bible has a footnote that says the correct translation for the phrase "you shall surely die" is "dying, you shall die". That is a very accurate translation because two deaths were involved. One happened that day and the other did not happen for nearly a millennium. "And the days that Adam lived were nine hundred and thirty years: and he died" (Genesis 5:5).

God created man a soul in a body. "And the Lord God formed man of the dust of the ground and breathed into his nostrils the breath of life; and man became a living soul" (Genesis 2:7). The body was physical, the same substance as the earth. But the soul was an individual existence. The Hebrew word translated soul is "nephesh", an existence that is individual – a personal will, mind, and heart – but which receives its nature from an outside source. "Nephesh" translated soul and the Hebrew word "Ruach" translated spirit can both be translated "breath" but Ruach is a forcible breath breathed out while nephesh is a breath breathed in. The breath of life breathed into man was God's Word about him, the concept expressed of "in our image after our likeness, and let them have dominion..." (Genesis 1:26). The soul was alive with God's Spirit, His own nature of goodness, authority over the physical realm, and power to bring his will to pass.

When mankind made a wrong choice, that choice had to do with only one part of the soul....the heart. But that part, the essential character, affects all the other parts.

The will did not change nature...whatever mankind wanted to do, they still had the power to do; we see God affirming that after the fall during the occasion of the building of the Tower of Babel. "...nothing will be restrained from them, which they have imagined to do" (Genesis 11:6).

The mind did not change nature...whatever was input into it set the course of the will. Paul confirmed this as he wrote, "Be not conformed to this world; but be transformed by the renewing of your mind..."(Romans 12:2). When our minds are conformed to the world it causes our will to be the world's will. When our minds are renewed to God's truth, it causes our wills to want His will.

The heart changed nature. "The heart is deceitful above all things, and desperately wicked. Who can know it" (Jeremiah 17:9)? When original man chose pollution, the heart of man was no longer connected to the character of God, no longer one with Love Himself. Yes, man was made in His image but chose pollution of character, "knowledge of both good and evil". We know, or perceive and are one with, both good and evil concepts. And we often do not know the difference.

Once some students of mine who were reading through the Bible for the first time came to me on the same day with horror concerning the family of Abraham's nephew Lot as told in Genesis 19. They asked "Why did Lot's wife get turned into salt for looking back at Sodom and yet his daughters got him drunk and had intercourse with him and nothing happened to them?" Immediately the Lord placed in my mind the answer to this seeming injustice and I explained, "Because there had been no law given against incest. There had been a command given about looking back at Sodom. And because of our fallen nature we don't know right from wrong unless it is told us."

This is one of the reasons that the Bible exists. "For as the rain comes down....that it may give seed to the sower and bread to the eater...so shall my word be that goes forth out of my mouth; it shall not return to me void, but it shall accomplish that which I please and it shall prosper in the thing that I sent it for"(Isaiah 55:10,11).

God gives His Word to us as a "lamp unto our feet, and a light unto our path" (Psalm 119:105). And because He is the Creator, His Words...His expressed concepts, ideas, and thoughts, are living Seed that grow up and come to pass wherever they are planted and nurtured.

We have seen the Law...the rules about right and wrong... as God's greatest good. But Paul tells us that "the law was our schoolmaster to bring us to Christ, that we might be justified by faith"(Galatians 3:24). God wants us to trust that He has taken care of the requirements of the law through Jesus Christ and that now we are restored, through faith in the work of Jesus Christ, to oneness with Him. We are to work that inner oneness outward, "Work out your own salvation with fear and trembling for it is God which works in you both to will and to do of His good pleasure" (Philippians 2:12,13).

From the time that Chaos – disconnectedness and disorder – came into the physical realm, God has been working to restore Peace...perfect wholeness in three realms.........spirit, soul, and body. The Spirit of Christ, the spirit of Sonship submitted to the Father, came into our souls when we invited Him in, and now we are to work that new character outwards submitting every part of our hearts to the Father, working that submission through our minds and wills and out into our bodies and circumstances.

JESUS TAUGHT US HIS PRAYER FOR PEACE

Jesus taught us to pray "Thy Kingdom come, Thy will be done on earth as it is in heaven" (Matthew 6:10). That is a prayer for Peace, for Shalom, for interconnectedness, wholeness, completeness, oneness.

Our opening scripture for this chapter was "And the very God of peace sanctify you wholly; and I pray God your whole spirit and soul and body be preserved blameless unto the coming of our Lord Jesus Christ" (I Thessalonians 5:23).

Chaos will completely end on earth when Jesus comes back and establishes the Kingdom of God here. But in the meantime He is in the process of working toward that goal. He sent the Holy Spirit to work peace in us, making us one with Himself as we look to Him and see ourselves born anew into His image and "are changed from glory to glory into the same image" (II Corinthians 3:18).

The definition of Glory is God's nature and acts in self manifestation.

When you were born again, you became a part of the glory of God, the manifestation of His nature. As you let His nature have place in your mind, will, and heart you are manifesting more and more of that nature to the world, changed into His image from one degree of glory to another (II Cor. 3:18)"

Peter says that we can hasten that day of the Lord by our behavior, as we submit to the Lord's life and character within us (II Peter 3:11.12). Paul says that Jesus will present His Church to Himself glorious, "not having spot, or wrinkle, or any such thing; but that it should be holy and without blemish" (Eph. 5:27).

All battles come as a part of the great War against Chaos...against disconnectedness and confusion....first in our souls as we reconnect spiritually with our Creator-heart, mind, and will. Then the natural outcome is Peace in our bodies and circumstances.

THINGS TO REMEMBER

The War

1. All battles are part of the war against chaos.

2. God is in the process of restoring wholeness.

3. You are God's vehicle of working in the earth.

4. God's Word comes to pass in your life as you receive it.

Scripture Truths

"And the very God of peace sanctify you wholly; and I pray God your whole spirit and soul and body be preserved blameless unto the coming of our Lord Jesus Christ."
I Th. 5:23

"For I know the thoughts that I think toward you, says the Lord, thoughts of peace, and not of evil..." Jeremiah 29:13

"Let us make man in our image after our likeness, and let them have dominion..." Genesis 1:26

"Be not conformed to this world; but be transformed by the renewing of your mind.." Romans 12:2

"Work out your own salvation with fear and trembling for it is God which works in you both to will and to do of His good pleasure." Philippians 2:12,13

47

"Christ will present His church to Himself clean by the washing of the water of the Word ...not having spot, or wrinkle, or any such thing; but that it should be holy and without blemish."   Ephesians 5:26, 27

WHOSOEVER IS BORN OF GOD OVERCOMES THE WORLD AND THIS IS THE VICTORY THAT OVERCOMES THE WORLD, OUR FAITH.   I John 5:4

Chapter Five

The Battle Against Unforgiveness

*"For if you forgive men their trespasses, your heavenly Father
will also forgive you; but if you forgive not men their
trespasses, neither will your Father forgive your trespasses."*
Matthew 6:14,15

This passage of scripture that follows the Lord's Prayer
is startling and frightening. Doesn't God forgive
everybody? Isn't it true that all we have to do is confess
our sins and receive His forgiveness (I John 1:9)?

Didn't Jesus speak out forgiveness from the cross for
all mankind (Luke 23:34)?

What does He mean by saying "if you don't forgive
men their sins against you, your Father will not forgive
your sins." ???

Jesus even goes farther in Chapter 18 of Matthew when
He tells a story about a man who owed the King a huge
amount of money and begged the King to be patient while
he worked to repay it. The King had compassion on him
and forgave the entire debt. But that man went out and
found someone who owed him a little bit of money and
demanded repayment. When the second debtor begged
for patience, he refused and had him thrown into prison.

When the King heard this, he put the debt back on the first man (Matt. 18:22 – 34).

After Jesus told this story He went on to say, "So shall my heavenly Father do to you if you, from your hearts, do not forgive every one his brother their trespasses" (Matt. 18:35). After being forgiven, the first man lost that forgiveness by refusing to forgive others.

Scary!

What does it mean?

This chapter is the most important chapter in this book and, I believe, the most important teaching needed by the Church, the Body of Christ in the earth.

I don't know the full extent of the implications in Jesus' teaching about forgiveness and that is not what this book is about. But I do know that one of the main components of spiritual warfare is forgiveness. It is the first battle that must be won before the successful completion of other battles.

In Mark 11: 22 – 26, Jesus gives a classic teaching on faith and receiving from God. "And Jesus answered them and said "Have faith in God. For truly I say to you that whosoever shall say to this mountain, Be removed and cast into the sea and shall not doubt in his heart, but shall believe that those things which he says shall come to pass; he shall have whatsoever he says. Therefore I say to you that whatsoever things you desire, when you pray believe that you receive them and you shall have them. **And when you stand praying forgive, if you have anything against anybody, so that your Father which is in heaven may forgive your trespasses. But if you do not forgive, neither will your Father which is in heaven forgive your trespasses."**

Forgiveness is an essential part of receiving from God. Jesus taught us to pray "Forgive us our trespasses as we forgive those who trespass against us" (Matthew 6:12).

We say the words, but do we really, truly, realize what we are asking?

Can you honestly with all your heart say "God, forgive all my wrongs in the same way that I forgive the wrongs done to me?"

Can I honestly say that?

There are many times I do not want God to forgive me in the same way I forgive others. I want His mercy to me to be complete; I don't want Him to withhold good things until the time that I repent, grovel, make good, pay back, get punished, admit my faults to the whole world. Surely none of us ever wanted those things from the ones who have harmed us, have we?

Shakespeare spoke through the words of Portia in Merchant of Venice, "The quality of mercy is not strained. It droppeth as the gentle rain from heaven upon the place beneath: it is twice bless'd; it blesseth him that gives and him that takes.......Though justice be thy plea consider this, that in the course of justice none of us should see salvation: we do pray for mercy, and that same prayer doth teach us all to render the deeds of mercy."

I wish Portia had been right when she said (at least I think this is what she said in her Elizabethan English) that we pray for mercy for ourselves and that prayer teaches us to be merciful to others. Unfortunately, most of us are not so wise as Portia. We want mercy for ourselves, but we want judgment and justice for others. And according to our Lord and Savior Jesus Christ, that is just what we cannot have.

We choose judgment and justice for all or we choose grace and mercy for all. God hates evil and He has spoken out against it. But he loves every person even when they are a vessel for that evil. We speak of hating the sin but loving the sinner, but most of the time we want to see the sinner pay for their sin, even though we want mercy for ourselves. We can't have it both ways; we must choose justice for self and others, or mercy for self and others.

Those who are demanding justice may find that they get it.

When we are crying out to God for His vengeance and repayment for wrongs done to us, we are putting ourselves on the opposite side of the fence from mercy and forgiveness. And when we are on the opposite side from mercy and forgiveness, we are exposing ourselves to judgment and justice, to vengeance and repayment for wrongs done by us. It's not God's choice; it is our choice.

JESUS PAID THE PRICE FOR ALL THE SINS OF ALL MANKIND IN ALL TIMES AND IN ALL PLACES.

Do we receive that as true or don't we? We can't pick and choose where we want that payment to apply or not apply. If it applies for me, it applies for everyone. If it doesn't apply to everyone, it doesn't apply to me. Jesus either paid for all your sins and all my sins or He didn't pay for all the sins of either of us.

Forgiveness is your most important action in spiritual warfare. You need to receive it and you need to give it.

If you are fighting the enemy for something for yourself, for health or provision or freedom from oppression or failure, you have to know that you are right in the eyes of God. Without that knowledge you are vulnerable to feelings of shame and unworthiness, and will have no strength to have faith in God's promises to you. The "Breastplate of Righteousness", mentioned in Ephesians 6 as one of the weapons of spiritual warfare, one of the parts of the armor of God, is the result of receiving the forgiveness which puts you in right standing with God. Your heart is protected by faith in His love for you – in His mercy that results in forgiveness. Most of the people I know who are experiencing terrible ongoing trials usually have some degree of belief that God has not really forgiven them for some sin they have committed.

"The quality of mercy is not strained; it droppeth as the gentle rain from heaven."... God has poured out mercy upon all mankind. The Holy Spirit who has been poured out on all flesh is called the Spirit of Grace (Hebrews 10: 29). Grace means undeserved favor - blessings given without cause - unearned benefits.

I used to have my car insurance with a company that gave me a "grace period" of a month. This meant that I was covered by insurance for a month after my payment period ended. I received an undeserved benefit.

Mercy goes a step farther than Grace, a step farther than just giving undeserved benefits. Mercy gives benefits when punishment is deserved.

Mercy was proclaimed when "God was in Christ, reconciling the world to himself, not imputing their trespasses to them; and He has committed to us the word of reconciliation" (II Corinthians 5:19).

We are to say with joy "No, I deserve nothing but I receive everything because of the mercy and grace of my Lord to me."

And we are to say with joy "No, you deserve nothing from me but I give you everything because of the mercy and grace of our Lord in and through me to you."

Can we say either? Can we say both?

Your enemy the devil hopes you cannot. He hates the mercy and grace of God more than anything in all heaven and earth. He is named "the accuser of our brethren" (Revelation 12:10). He is continually accusing mankind. He accuses you to yourself and others, and he accuses others to you and themselves. He wants above all to distract us from the grace of God as shown on the cross of Calvary. We are told how he is overcome..."by the blood of the Lamb, and by the word of our testimony" (Revelation 12:11). The blood of the Lamb paid for sin and washes us clean from sin. And the word of our testimony is that God is not holding the sin of anybody against them but reaches out with love and mercy and blessing. That is the essence of the Gospel, the Good News.

The devil will fight to keep you from receiving and giving forgiveness more than any other spiritual benefit and blessing. If he can keep you from understanding the completeness of God's love and mercy, he can hinder the correct picture of God from being seen in the earth, and he can keep deceiving you and the world so that his will is accepted as God's will.

God longs for you to understand Who He is and that He is not holding your sin against you. The cry of His heart was written in Hosea 6:6: "**For I desired mercy, and not sacrifice; and the knowledge of God more than burnt offerings.**" He longs for you to know that He is the same yesterday, today, and forever. He never was holding the sins of mankind against them but was working, working, working, to get mankind to receive His instrument of grace so that reconciliation could take place. "The law was our schoolmaster to bring us to Christ, so that we might be justified by faith" (Gal. 3:24).

A few years ago when I was praying about why we don't see healings and miracles happen as often as I know God wants them to happen, I had a vision flash into my mind. I saw a floodwall made up of many little bricks. Behind the floodwall was a huge ocean pounding against the floodwall, but it couldn't break through. Then I saw that the ocean was the Holy Spirit and His gifts. And the floodwall was built, brick by brick, of the unforgiveness, criticism, and judgmentalness............in the Body of Christ!

What a shock! It was not the sins of the worldly people that were holding back the demonstrations of God's love and mercy and grace. It was the lack of love and mercy and grace in His Body in the earth, the Christians, lack of love in the ones equipped and empowered to be vessels of that love.

Each little brick was a judgment, an anger, a bitterness that stopped the flow of the Holy Spirit. I was appalled and grieved and ashamed, knowing that I too had placed some of the bricks in the wall. And I felt hopeless. If the problem was in the answer, if the salt of the earth has lost its savor, if the light of the world has been extinguished, what could be done? Then I saw a hand placing sticks of dynamite in the wall. And I saw other hands lighting the sticks of dynamite. And where the dynamite exploded, the bricks were blasted into little pieces, and there at those places the water gushed forth. And I understood that the sticks of dynamite were teachings on forgiveness, and where they were received and implemented, the manifestations of God's love could pour out in the earth.

How could this be that the Body of Christ has such power to hinder the Spirit of God? It is because God has ordained that He work through His Body in the earth. Jesus Christ is the Vine and we are the branches; He is the Head and we are the Body.

We have not yet gotten the revelation of our mission and our importance to the ministry of the Lord Jesus Christ. We are it. There is no Plan B.

Weeks before the Day of Pentecost when Jesus poured out the Spirit of Grace from heaven on all flesh and filled His Body in the earth with fire, on the very day He was raised from the dead, He did something for those whom He called his own. He breathed into His own the new creation nature, the Spirit of Christ, the nature of Sonship of the Father God who is Love. He said "As the Father has sent me, even so I am sending you. Receive the Holy Spirit; whoever's sins you remit, they are remitted; and whoever's sins you retain, they are retained" (John 20:21-23).

Can you grasp that? Can you believe that you have the power on earth to forgive sins? Can you see that is what the apostle Paul was talking about when he said, in II Corinthians 5:19, that God has committed to us the word of reconciliation? "God was in Christ reconciling the world unto himself, not imputing their trespasses unto them; and has committed unto us the word of reconciliation."

If we don't take that word of reconciliation, the truth that God was in Christ not imputing the sins of the world to them, the truth doesn't get taken, the word doesn't get said, reconciliation doesn't happen.

God was in Christ, reconciling the world to Himself, not imputing their sins to them. The word impute, according to The American Heritage Dictionary is "to ascribe a crime or fault to another" and "to attribute to a cause or source." God was in Christ on the cross not attributing the sins of mankind to them.

God does not ascribe the crimes and faults to the humans who are doing them.

God is perfect at hating the sin and loving the sinner. He has no desire to punish the ones who have allowed sin to operate through them; He only wants to set them free from the sin that torments and drives them. God has attributed the crimes and faults of mankind to a single source, the devil.

Can you do the same thing? Can you agree with God? Can you attribute your own sins to the devil and believe that God loves you completely and has paid the cost for your sin?

Can you attribute the sins of the one who has damaged you most in life to the devil and believe that God loves that person completely and has paid the cost for their sin?

We are asking God to save people and at the same time we are praying that they reap the consequences of their sin so they will turn to God.

I hear people all the time saying that some bad thing is happening "for a reason". The philosophy behind that belief is that God is causing, or allowing, some bad thing to happen so the person involved will finally come to their senses.

I am seeing more and more clearly the "reason" that the bad things are happening. It is because we, the Body of Christ, haven't held forth the word of reconciliation that says that God is not imputing the sin to the person and that God wants to bless them.

In Paul's teaching about judging, he says "wherein you judge another, you condemn yourself...do you despise the riches of His goodness and forbearance and longsuffering, not knowing that the goodness of God leads you to repentance" (Romans 2:1-4)? If only we could get a revelation of that! It is God's goodness that leads us to repentance, His goodness as demonstrated by His patience and His love and His mercy and grace toward us. And it is God's goodness that will lead others to repentance.

Do you want somebody to repent? Bless them. Bless them with your words and bless them with actions. Show them the goodness of God.

I have given Anger Resolution Workshops several times over the past few years. In those workshops we look at the underlying causes of anger and at the manifestations of anger.

Always, the resolution to anger is forgiveness – both receiving and giving forgiveness. Always we find that one of the biggest problems we Christians have is a misunderstanding about what forgiveness is and what it isn't.

Forgiveness is not excusing sin. I realized only a few years ago that even though I had thought I was forgiving everyone, sometimes I didn't actually forgive because I was excusing the bad behavior, saying the person didn't really understand what they were doing or they didn't mean to be so hurtful. But the Lord finally showed me that wrong hurtful actions are sin and need to be called that. Sin needs to be seen as what it is – evil. Only when we see it and name it can we really forgive the person who was responsible for it . **Forgiveness is to assign the punishment for the wrong act to the cross, agreeing that Jesus' sacrifice was sufficient to meet the claims of justice.** And after you forgive, you are to speak accordingly, not speaking excuses for them or, on the other hand, talking about how they need to be punished for what they did to you.

Forgiveness is not saying it's okay. The world says, "time heals all wounds". But that is not true. Only Jesus can heal all wounds. Time just buries unhealed wounds more deeply in our hearts. We often say, "it doesn't matter anymore". But if the wound you received has not been healed, it does still matter and it is affecting your emotions even when you don't realize it. Forgiveness means saying that the hurts of the past can't affect the present or the future because Jesus meets all your emotional needs. **Forgiveness is putting the sin and pain in the past, and making Jesus Lord over the future.**

Forgiveness is not a restored relationship. Once I had a pastor who kept doing things that hurt me over and over. And over and over I would forgive him and try to have a harmonious relationship with him. Finally one day I went to the Lord and asked what the problem was. I said "I think I have forgiven but the relationship is not right so I must be doing something wrong. Please show me." And immediately I had a mental picture of Jesus on the cross saying "Father, forgive them..." And then the Lord communicated to me, "I forgive everyone again and again but until a person recognizes their need for My forgiveness and wants a harmonious relationship with Me, the forgiveness I give does not change the relationship." We are to do our part. We can't do the other person's part too, nor can we demand it as a condition of our forgiveness. Forgiveness is not given conditionally but unconditionally.

I forgave the pastor again and from that time on I did not feel personally wounded by his treatment of me. Our relationship never became harmonious but it did eventually cease to be unpleasant.

Forgiveness is agreeing with grace. Forgiveness means agreeing that, even if the person has not recognized their need for your forgiveness, even if they do not want a relationship with you, you agree with God's grace for them.

Forgiveness is done with the will and confirmed with the mouth. The initial forgiveness is an act of your will, and the continued and ongoing agreements with forgiveness are also acts of your will. The confirmation of the initial forgiveness is to speak out loud that you have forgiven the person. The confirmation of your continued forgiveness is that you never speak badly of the person or the situation again.

Forgiveness is important to you in your own prayer life. You need to receive forgiveness from God and get rid of unforgiveness toward others so that you can receive your prayers answered.

Forgiveness is important to your salvation because you choose judgment or mercy for self as you choose for others. If you are choosing judgment instead of mercy, you cannot receive what God wants to pour out freely because of His mercy.

Forgiveness is crucial to your Christian walk. Forgiveness is the very thing you are called to do.

When you can walk in forgiveness – for self and others– the key battle preceding any other battle of spiritual warfare is won, the main fighting ground is taken from the enemy.

Remember:

Forgiveness is not excusing sin; forgiveness is assigning the punishment for the sin to the cross.

Forgiveness is not saying that everything is all right now; forgiveness is putting the sin in the past and refusing to let it affect you emotionally by letting Jesus heal your broken heart.

Forgiveness is not a restored relationship; forgiveness is agreeing with God's grace for the person who hurt you.

FORGIVENESS IS DONE WITH THE WILL AND CONFIRMED WITH THE MOUTH!

THINGS TO REMEMBER

The Battle Against Unforgiveness

1. You need to forgive in order to receive forgiveness.

2. The devil is the accuser; God is the justifier. With whom do you agree?

3. Proclaiming forgiveness is the main responsibility of the Body of Christ.

4. Forgiveness is done with the will and confirmed with the mouth.

Scripture Truths

"For if you forgive men their trespasses, your heavenly Father will also forgive you; But if you forgive not men their trespasses, neither will your Father forgive your trespasses."
Matthew 6:14,15

"wherein you judge another, you condemn yourself.....do you despise the riches of His goodness and forbearance and longsuffering, not knowing that the goodness of God leads you to repentance?" Romans 2: 1-4

"As the Father has sent me, even so I am sending you. Receive the Holy Spirit; whoever's sins you remit, they are remitted; and whoever's sins you retain, they are retained."
John 20:21-23

AND GRIEVE NOT THE HOLY SPIRIT OF GOD, WHEREBY YOU ARE SEALED UNTO THE DAY OF

REDEMPTION. LET ALL BITTERNESS, AND WRATH, AND ANGER, AND CLAMOUR, AND EVIL SPEAKING BE PUT AWAY FROM YOU, WITH ALL MALICE; AND BE KIND, TENDERHEARTED, FORGIVING ONE ANOTHER, EVEN AS GOD FOR CHRIST'S SAKE HAS FORGIVEN YOU. Ephesians 4:30-32

Chapter Six

The Battle Against Depression

"...When my heart is overwhelmed, lead me to the rock that is higher than I."

Psalm 61:2

According to Webster's New World Dictionary, to be overwhelmed is to be "poured down on and buried beneath" and to be "crushed and overpowered".

There are times in the lives of all of us when our hearts have been flooded by some heartrending circumstance until we are buried beneath the resulting sorrow and left gasping for breath. There are times when we are crushed and overpowered and left in a state of emotional paralysis. At those times we cannot see beyond sorrow to a time of future peace and joy.

Psalm 61 is attributed to David but we do not know under which overwhelming circumstance in his life it was written. At the moment when his heart was overwhelmed and his will paralyzed, he cried out "lead me to the rock that is higher than I". He knew that he was incapable, left to himself, of even reaching the shelter of God's presence. It was one of those times where, like Jonah in the belly of

63

the great fish, his soul had "fainted within" and he cried out for help (Jonah 2:7).

It is interesting that David recognized that he was incapable of getting to the place of shelter, the "Rock" higher than himself, on his own. He cried out for someone to lead him there. And we know that the Someone who leads us to the Rock, the Savior, the Redeemer who is the Lord Jesus Christ, is the Holy Spirit of God (John 16:13-15).

David lived before the day of Pentecost when the Holy Spirit was poured out on all flesh. He was able to recognize the availability of the Holy Spirit's leading because he was a descendent of Abraham and a part of the covenant between God and Abraham.

From the day of Pentecost, the Holy Spirit has been available to every human being. When we cry out for help, we are actually crying out for God to lead us to God, for Him to take the responsibility to bring us up out of the pit of despair and the mire of self-pity. And He does. David says in Psalm 40: 2, "He brought me up out of an horrible pit, out of the miry clay, and set my feet upon a rock, and established my goings."

God did it for David and He did it for Jonah. He did it for Paul and Silas when they sang praises to Him in the midst of a prison cell after being severely beaten (Acts 16:22 – 26). And He will do it for you.

In Galatians 3:13 we are promised that Jesus bore the curse for us. The curse is a list of those things that happen as a consequence of not obeying God's law. And not one of us perfectly obeys God's law. There is that part inside of us that knows we deserve the curse because we know ourselves to be sinners. But Jesus redeemed us from those consequences by taking them into His own body. Among those consequences listed as results of breaking God's law are "a trembling heart, and failing of eyes, and sorrow of mind; and thy life shall hang in doubt before thee; and thou shalt fear day and night, and shalt have no assurance of thy life. In the morning thou shalt say, 'Would God it were evening' and in the evening thou shalt say 'Would God it were morning'...." (Deut. 28:65-67). That sound like classic depression to me!

Depression is viewing life as misery. Depression is hopeless about the future. Depression is fear and defeat. Depression is the complete absence of joy.

Joy knows that life will get better. Joy is filled with hope and faith. Joy sees victory in the future. We are told that Jesus "for the joy that was set before him endured the cross..." (Hebrews 12:2).

If you have received Jesus as your Savior, you are redeemed from depression and you have that same joy available to you!

A promise to those who have accepted Jesus is that they will be given "the oil of joy for mourning and the garment of praise for the spirit of heaviness" (Isaiah 61:3).

Depression, the spirit of heaviness, is not God's will for you!

Like David you can cry out for the Holy Spirit to lead you to the Rock that is Jesus Christ and be hidden in His life. His life is the resurrection life that is "far above all principality, and power, and might, and dominion, and every name that is named, not only in this world but also in that which is to come" (Ephesians 1:21). For that is the truth of who and where you are in Christ Jesus.

Depression comes from a perception that the world and the devil are more real and more powerful than God and the Blood of Jesus that redeems us from sorrow into joy. Depression is often combined with idolatry of some kind - thinking that the thing we wanted and didn't get is the only thing that can make us happy, and thus refusing the joy that comes from Him. This sort of thinking leads to hopelessness that is the very basis of depression.

Those perceptions are as much a lie from the enemy as the lie told to Adam in the garden. You are called, like the first man and woman, to stay connected to the Tree of Life and not partake of the "knowledge of both good and evil" (Genesis 1: 16,17; 2:1-7). We in the church of the Lord Jesus Christ are guilty of the same offense – believing the lies of the enemy and filling ourselves with his reactions to life instead of believing the promises and warnings of God. We are to fix our hearts on the Lord, trusting in His loving care and promises. When we do that, the purposes of the devil cannot prosper (Psalm 112: 7 – 10).

Depression is often anger turned inward when the enemy has convinced us that we should hate ourselves, that we deserve bad things to happen because of some action we did or left undone - or worse, because of some flaw in our character or personality. That is a lie; there is only one correct target of anger, the devil, the accuser of the brethren, the father of lies, the adversary.

When we refuse to see things his way, when we refuse to believe what he tells us about who we are and the "end of the story" in our circumstances, when we turn to the Father of mercy and truth and set ourselves to believe Him and see things His way, depression cannot stay with us. When we forgive ourselves for not being perfect, when we receive our forgiveness from God, we can recognize that there is hope for our future.

In Nehemiah 8:10 we read "…neither be ye sorry, for the joy of the Lord is your strength."

WHAT IS THE JOY OF THE LORD?

The Joy of the Lord is God's own emotion concerning circumstances because He knows the end of the story – Joy is the result of His faith. Joy is God's assurance that the thing He hopes for will come to pass (Hebrews 11:1). Jesus endured the cross "for the joy that was set before Him" (Hebrews 12:2). He was able to go through what He went through for you and me because He believed in the outcome. And what He was believing in was your freedom and holiness and joy, my freedom and holiness and joy.

We are told to "set your affection on things above, not on things on the earth" (Col. 3:3). That is because as we look to heavenly things we see clearly what God wants to happen on earth. Jesus taught us to pray "Thy will be done on earth as it is in heaven" (Matthew 6:10). If we don't know what is happening in heaven, then we can't agree with it and know what God wants to happen in the earth.

What is happening in heaven is that you are "blessed with all spiritual blessing in heavenly places in Christ" (Ephesians 1:3). And God wants His will done on earth as it is in heaven.

When your heart is overwhelmed and you cry out "Lead me to the Rock that is higher than I!" you are asking God for His perspective on your circumstances and He always sees victory because He bought and paid for it and knows that it will come to pass as you receive it.

No wonder David could say "I will be glad and rejoice in thee; I will sing praise to thy name, O thou most High. When mine enemies are turned back, they shall fall and perish at thy presence" (Psalm 9: 2,3). When we praise God for being the victor, we bring His victory on the scene; when we praise God for being the healer, we bring healing on the scene; when we praise God for being our provider, we bring provision on the scene. When we praise God for Himself, we bring His joy on the scene.

It is not easy to praise God in the middle of painful circumstances. The writer of Hebrews tells us to offer the "sacrifice of praise" (Hebrews 13:15). Praise is a sacrifice when we are feeling defeat and sorrow. But when we do it, the enemy, who is the source of defeat and sorrow, truly does fall back and perish at His Presence.

"In Your Presence is fullness of joy" (Psalm 16:11), and when we set our minds to see His mind and we put His victory in our mouths, we are choosing His presence and when He is present, joy drives out sorrow just as light drives out darkness.

Once I was listening to a gospel song about seeing Jesus in heaven and suddenly I had a mental picture of Jesus' head and shoulders with a street and buildings in the background. His face was radiant with joy. And I knew that if sorrow tried to come there on that street it would dissolve in the presence of His joy in the same way that darkness cannot come into a lighted room.

Depression is your enemy and it is the enemy of God's Word. You can fight symptoms of depression with drugs, but only God's Truth and God's Joy can drive it out of your heart and mind. If you have a chemical imbalance that causes depression, by all means take your medication until and unless the Lord does a physical miracle and balances the chemical makeup in your body.

There are many people on anti-depressants that do not need to be on them, whose depression problems are not caused by a chemical imbalance. And there are many people with chemical imbalances who are on medication and yet have no joy in their lives because physical medicine cannot cure spiritual problems.

Joy is a fruit of the Spirit. You can't replace depression with joy because it is not a fruit of your will, or a fruit of your personality. Joy is a fruit of the Spirit of God. As you allow more of the Holy Spirit in your life, He will drive out depression with joy.

Joy is all about triumph and victory in life. Depression is all about hopelessness and failure in life.

When your heart is overwhelmed, turn to the one who overwhelms your sorrow with His joy. Depression melts away at the presence of joy.

When depression melts away, anger finds it's correct target and turns outward on the devil, the Father of lies, who has deceived you into believing wrong things about yourself and God and life.

God has great things planned for you, "For I know the thoughts that I think toward you, says the Lord, thoughts of peace, and not of evil, to give you hope and a future" (Jeremiah 29:11).

So what is the practical application of this knowledge?

Praise Him! He gives us the garment of praise for the spirit of heaviness. The spirit of heaviness cannot stay in the same place as the garment of praise. You take the garment of praise, put His promises in your mouth, speak joyfully of His nature and the spirit of heaviness must leave. It will leave, and the Lord's victory will be seen in your life.

Put on praise and worship music; read Psalms aloud; speak of all the wonderful things He has done in your life.

Remember Spiritual Warfare Principle #2:

PRAISE OF GOD BRINGS GOD ON THE SCENE

THINGS TO REMEMBER

The Battle Against Depression

1. Depression is anger turned inward.

2. Depression is not God's will for you. He loves you and has good things planned for your future.

3. Only God can lead you out of depression.

4. Joy is a fruit of the spirit and comes only from God's presence in your life.

5. Praising God brings God's presence to your circumstances.

Scripture Truths

"...When my heart is overwhelmed, lead me to the rock that is higher than I."   Psalm 61:2

"In His Presence is fullness of joy and at His right hand there are pleasures forever."   Psalm 16:11

"I will be glad and rejoice in thee; I will sing praise to thy name, O thou most High. When mine enemies are turned back, they shall fall and perish at thy presence."   Psalm 9: 2,3

"...neither be ye sorry, for the joy of the Lord is your strength."
                                                        Nehemiah 8:10

"The Spirit of the Lord God is upon me because the Lord has anointed me to preach good tidings to the meek; he has sent me to bind up the brokenhearted, to proclaim liberty to the captives, and the opening of the prison to them that are bound; to

proclaim the acceptable day of the Lord and the day of vengeance of our God; to comfort all that mourn; to appoint unto them that mourn in Zion, to give them beauty for ashes, the oil of joy for mourning, the garment of praise for the spirit of heaviness; that they might be called trees of righteousness, the planting of the Lord, that he might be glorified."

Isaiah 61:1-3

MANY SAY OF MY SOUL 'THERE IS NO HELP FOR HIM IN GOD,' BUT THOU, O LORD ARE A SHIELD FOR ME; MY GLORY AND THE LIFTER UP OF MY HEAD. Psalm 3:2,3

Chapter Seven

The Battle Against Anxiety

"My brethren, count it all joy when you fall into divers temptations; knowing this, that the trying of your faith works patience. But let patience have her perfect work, that you may be perfect and entire, wanting nothing."

James 1:2-4

The word translated "temptations" is peirasmos in the original Greek and it means a putting to proof, or a testing.

Count it all joy when you fall into different temptations? Count it joy when you are in the midst of testings? Has the author of the book of James lost his mind?

Who in their right mind could "count it joy" to be in the middle of an uncomfortable situation that tests your faith, something so important that it will prove what you really believe and who you really trust?

Who could count it all joy?

The Christian who is wise, that's who. But this takes some understanding.

According to the American Heritage Dictionary, the word anxiety means "a state of uneasiness and distress about future uncertainties; apprehension; worry".

Who has not at some time been anxious concerning the future? Who has not felt unease and distress about something that may or may not happen? Who has not been apprehensive about some upcoming event? Who has never worried?

If you can answer "Me" to those questions, this chapter is not for you.

But most of us cannot answer "me" to any of them. All of us have had times of anxiety. Some of us have had many terrible times of anxiety. A few of us live in a state of anxiety.

But anxiety is an enemy. It is an enemy to you and to the God of Peace. "Be <u>careful</u> for nothing; but in everything by prayer and supplication with thanksgiving let your requests be made known to God. And the peace of God, which passes all understanding shall keep your hearts and minds through Christ Jesus" (Philippians 4:6,7).

The word translated "careful" is the Greek "merimnao" and means "to be anxious". God's Word tells us that we are not supposed to be anxious about anything. We are not to worry, we are not to be apprehensive, we are not to be uneasy or distressed about the future.

Why?

And how?

We looked at the battle against depression and saw that a large ingredient of depression is hopelessness, the lack of hope toward future happiness. Anxiety includes some depression but the main component of anxiety is fear. Anxiety is not only lacking in hope of good things concerning the future, as is depression, but it fears that bad things, even worse things than are happening in the present, will happen in the future.

The two words "Fear not!" occur together 99 times in the Bible. That injunction is given more than any other directive from God.

FEAR NOT! And if God tells us not to do it, then we have the ability to obey that command.

I remember one time when I was in the heat of the battle concerning full time ministry, fighting the wrong scriptural interpretations and cultural prejudices against women preachers, not just in society but in my own heart and mind. I was sitting out in back of my house on the carport, surrounded by the first azaleas of the spring, with my Bible in my lap, weary from trying to sort out the voices in my own mind – what was me, what was the Holy Spirit, and what was the devil? I finally just closed my eyes and emotionally rested in His Presence. And then I had a mental vision.

I saw Jesus standing in front of me, smiling gently, with a bit of a twinkle in His eyes, as if He knew something I didn't know. He reached down and scooped something out of my heart and cupped it in His two hands. (Remember this is a mental vision!) I said, "What is it?" (with trepidation). He said nothing but opened His hands slightly so I could see. I leaned over and peered into His hands. And there was a little baby chicken. I immediately thought of the phrase "chicken hearted" and knew that it represented the fear in my heart of the opinions of others and what the future might hold if I followed what I knew the Holy Spirit was calling me to. I asked, "What can we do about it?" His smile grew bigger, He held up His arms, opened His hands completely, and the chicken flew away.

I know that chickens don't fly away into the sky and the Lord who created them certainly knows that. But it was an illustration of my deliverance from anxiety.

Did you notice what I did before the vision began? I stopped struggling mentally, and emotionally rested in His Presence. In other words, I trusted Him beyond my own reasoning and beyond the traditions of some branches of the Church and the opinions of others. I rested in His love for me, knowing that He cared about me and willed only good for me and that He could be trusted with my future.

I am convinced that being anxious is one of the greatest insults we can give our Lord and Savior. Being anxious is saying "I don't trust You! Not in this situation."

Peter wrote "Humble yourselves therefore under the mighty hand of God, that He may exalt you in due time: casting all your care upon Him; for He cares for you" (I Peter 5:6,7).

TO HUMBLE YOURSELF UNDER THE HAND OF GOD IS TO HAND HIM ALL YOUR CONCERNS ABOUT THE FUTURE...AND TRUST HIM TO DEAL WISELY AND LOVINGLY WITH THEM.

Easier said than done! But easier done the more you do it!

Your relationship with God – your personal, intimate, practical relationship with Him - is just like your relationship with any other person. You have to have experiences with a person in order to know whether you can trust them.

Most of us are so busy meeting our own needs that we never entrust anything to God and thus never discover that He is trustworthy. Many of us don't even know that God has called us to a personal, intimate, practical, interactive relationship with Himself.

If you and I are friends, how do you know if you can trust me? When you first meet me, you may think I am trustworthy but you don't really know until you have been in a position to need me to come through for you in some way that I have promised you can depend on me. Trust is based on a person giving their word about something and then following through on that word with action.

If you are disappointed in me over something I never promised to do or be for you, then the problem lies in your perception of our relationship. But if your disappointment in me is because I promised something and did not follow through on that promise, I am untrustworthy.

God has made some promises to you. You need to find out what they are and then "prove" His trustworthiness. "God is not a man, that He should lie, neither the son of man, that He should repent. Has He said, and shall He not do it? Or has He spoken, and shall He not make it good" (Numbers 23:19)?

God said that when you humble yourself to cast all your cares upon Him, He will exalt you. If you do your part, He will do His part. The enemy doesn't want us to believe that.

First he will get you to think God doesn't want you to bother Him with your cares, that you really need to take care of these things yourself with the resources of wisdom and provision God has already given you. The enemy tells you that true humility is to see your own needs as unimportant but if it is something you really have to have as a basic sustenance of life, then you should handle it yourself.

Then, if you refuse to believe the devil, and you go ahead and trust the Lord to care about and handle your problem, the enemy will then try to get you to take it back into your own control.

Remember what Paul wrote in Philippians 6: 6,7, We are to not be anxious about anything but take **everything** to God and when we have done this, it is God's own peace that protects our hearts and minds.

It is this process of casting our concerns into the hands of God and trusting Him with the future that Paul was speaking of in the opening scripture of this chapter.

"My brethren, count it all joy when you fall into divers temptations; knowing this, that the trying of your faith works patience. But let patience have her perfect work, that you may be perfect and entire, wanting nothing" (James 1:2-4).

The "trying of your faith" is the enemy's attempt to get you to not trust God with your problem. The patience spoken of is endurance. The enemy wants you to distrust God and take back the resolution of your problem into your own hands; he wants you to worry with it in your mind. But if you continually cast down those thoughts and say aloud, "That's God's concern now and I trust Him because He loves me", the voices of doubt and fear get fainter and fainter.

When you endure, hanging in there and trusting God no matter how you feel or what is bombarding your mind, when you refuse to mistrust God's love and His Word, then your faith grows stronger. Your experiential relationship with God is more solid. The foundation of your future trust is laid. Your trusting in and relying on God grows and brings you into a place where your life is complete, lacking nothing, because the Giver of all good gifts (James 1:17) is the Source of your every answer.

Put on the breastplate of righteousness, the breastplate of truth and love. Know that He loves you and that He will keep His promises to you. "There is no fear in love but perfect love casts out fear"(I John 4:18). His love for you is your protection and your deliverance.

Sometimes we experience unspecified anxiety caused by the stress of the modern world we live in. We can't think what promise to look for because we don't really know what the source of our anxiety is. These times are an indication that we have been too caught up in the world and we need a time of refreshing in His presence to renew our priorities and perspective.

Remember, if you are in Christ Jesus you are redeemed from "a trembling heart"(Deuteronomy 28:65, (Galatians 3:13). Jesus cried out on the cross, "My God, my God, why have you forsaken me?"(Matt. 27:46) bearing the forsaking, the aloneness, the anxiety that you deserve because of your sinfulness. And then He promised that you would never be forsaken. "Lo, I am with you always, even to the end of the world" (Matthew 28:20).

FEAR NOT!

"...for He has said 'I will never leave you, nor forsake you, so that we may boldly say, 'The Lord is my helper, and I will not fear what man shall do to me'" (Hebrews 13:5,6).

We may "boldly say". Don't forget that speaking aloud brings God on the scene and causes the enemy to be defeated by His Presence.

THINGS TO REMEMBER

The Battle Against Anxiety

1. Anxiety is fear; perfect Love casts out fear.

2. You have no reason for fear, for He promised to never leave you or forsake you.

3. You can trust God with your future because He loves you. Cast all your cares on Him and He will protect your heart and mind.

4. The devil wants you to distrust God's love and promises.

5. When you endure the battle against your faith, and keep God's Word in your mouth, and trust Him in your heart, you grow in perfection and will see the day when you lack no good thing.

Scripture Truths

"Humble yourselves therefore under the mighty hand of God, that He may exalt you in due time: casting all your care upon Him; for He cares for you."   I Pet. 5:6,7

"My brethren, count it all joy when you fall into divers temptations; knowing this, that the trying of your faith works patience. But let patience have her perfect work, that you may be perfect and entire, wanting nothing."   James 1:2-4

"...for He has said 'I will never leave you, nor forsake you, so that we may boldly say, 'The Lord is my helper, and I will not fear what man shall do to me.'"   Hebrews 13:5,6

"You are redeemed from…a trembling heart."
Deut. 28:65, Gal. 3:13

FOR GOD HAS NOT GIVEN US THE SPIRIT OF FEAR, BUT OF POWER AND OF LOVE, AND OF A SOUND MIND. II Timothy 1:7

Chapter Eight

The Battle Against Confusion

"If any of you lack wisdom, let him ask of God, that gives to all men liberally, and upbraids not; and it shall be given him."
James 1:5

"Which job should I take?"
"Which house should I buy?"
"Which church should I attend?"
"What diet and exercise program should I choose?"
"How strictly should I discipline my child / employee?"
"Should I do what the other person wants me to do, or what I want to do?"
"What do I really want anyway?"
"There are three things warring inside me. I want all of them."
"I don't want to do that - but I think I should."
"Eeny, meeny, miney, mo."

Do any of these questions or statements sound familiar? You are an unusual person if you have not had one or more of them running around your mind at some time or another.

Confusion, according to the New World Dictionary, is "a state of disorder, bewilderment, failure to distinguish between things". Bewilderment is "to have numerous conflicting situations, objects, or statements; to lose one's sense of where one is."

I liked the last two phrases in each definition – "failure to distinguish between things" and "to lose one's sense of where one is". They paint a picture of my own state of mind when I am confused and the state of mind of many people I have talked to when they are confused.

When I am confused, I cannot distinguish between whether something is good or bad, whether I should accept or reject. When I am confused I am not sure where I am, whether I am on a right path or a wrong path or no path at all.

When I am confused, I have a difficult time distinguishing the voice of God from the voice of the devil and from my own common sense and from my own will. And sometimes all four of those voices are going on in me.

For example, I am invited to go to a Christian meeting by my boss but I have promised to spend that evening with my husband. I am confused because:

1. I want to go to the meeting because I love to worship and I enjoy that kind of meeting.

2. My common sense tells me that going to the meeting will be good for my relationship with the person who invited me and could be beneficial to my future.

3. The devil tells me that if I don't go to the meeting, I will miss out on something God wants to give me, and I will go through life without that needed gift.

4. God tells me that I have given my word to my husband and that He has some important emotional healing for us to receive during that time.

But if I am confused, I wonder which voice is which. I don't know the voice of God from the voice of the devil or my own common sense.

How do I sort them out?

First, I ask God for His wisdom. I ask in faith, according to James 1:5, knowing that He wants to give me His wisdom.

Second, I spot the lie. The devil is the one who puts fear in my heart about God's nature. He tries to present God as a "get it now from Me or lose it forever" kind of God when the truth is that God is patient. Patience is the first of the virtues of Love defined in I Corinthians 13. God does not put a "now or never" type of emotional pressure on anyone. The devil's accusations against the love of God toward mankind are variations on the same theme he used successfully in the garden of Eden (Genesis 2:1-6). He always begins by painting God as a withholder instead of a generous giver. He always paints God as a liar and a legalist. I know that fear is never from God so that shows me that the compulsion to go out of fear of forever missing out on a blessing is not from Him.

Third, I see the Word of scripture that guides me. "As God is true, our word toward you was not yea and nay" (II Corinthians 1:17). God's Word tells me that if I have given my word of promise, I need to keep it.

Once I have distinguished between the voice of God and the voice of the devil, the other voices are easily distinguished. I see that I would rather go worship because there have been some tensions in my relationship with my husband that I would rather not confront. I see that even though I always love to worship God and sit under the Word, my biggest motive on this occasion is emotional safety.

When I have exposed that one wrong motive, I can remember that God is the one who gives me favor and advances my position in the Kingdom; I don't have to be a people pleaser for my future to be benefited. The other wrong motive is laid to rest.

The light of truth disperses confusion and shows me how the enemy was polluting even my will and my mind in order to bring his will to pass.

What?

WOULD THE DEVIL EVER SEND YOU TO A CHRISTIAN MEETING?

Of course he would, if the will of God is for you to be somewhere else.

A man once told me sadly that he'd stopped for gas on the way to church one day and the attendant asked if he could talk to him. My friend looked at his watch and said "Not now. I'm almost late for Sunday School." The next afternoon, he read in the newspaper that the gas station attendant had committed suicide that Sunday afternoon. Which was the most important appointment?

When I submit my will and mind to the will and mind of the Lord, the promise of God comes to pass. "For you shall go out with joy, and be led forth with peace..." (Isaiah 55:12). When a decision is made in harmony with God's will, peace will come along with it. When He is leading you, peace accompanies you. An orderly mind replaces a disordered one. If you don't have peace, stop right where you are and be willing to change your decision.

"And your ears shall hear a word behind you, saying 'This is the way, walk in it' when you turn to the right hand, and when you turn to the left" (Isaiah 30:21). God gave you free will and He will not make your choices for you. But He will confirm your choices with an inner "knowing" that you are on the right path.

The end of this particular attack of confusion is that God has His way and the problems in my marriage are resolved by Him in the time and place He chose. This does not mean He could have not done it at another time or place but my choice of honoring my word allowed Him to bring resolution sooner than later.

All confusion is from the devil. As we learned in the first chapter on the principles of spiritual warfare, he comes along with those things in our genetic makeup (in this case a desire to escape problems) and our cultural habits (people pleasing) to bring about his will (keeping me from receiving the resolution of my marital problems at that time). He also knew that since I would have been out of the will of God, the quality of my worship would have been polluted and God would have not received any joy from it. And I would not have been able to receive from God since what God wanted to give me at that time was waiting in another place. This was one of his schemes that we are warned against in Ephesians 6: 11 "Put on the whole armor of God, that you may be able to stand against the schemes of the devil."

We stand against the devil's schemes by arming ourselves with the Word of God. It is the Word of God in my heart that points out the lie concerning God's nature. It is the Word of God that shows me the area God wants to clear up in my life. It is the Word of God that shows me to trust Him for favor and advancement. It is the Word of God that shines light on the true motives of my heart.

"All scripture is given by inspiration of God, and is profitable for doctrine, for reproof, for correction, for instruction in righteousness: that the man of God may be perfect, thoroughly furnished unto all good works" (II Timothy 3:16,17).

It is the Word of God that disperses confusion and brings me peace. But sometimes I don't want to hear the Word and Will of God.

And if I truly don't want to hear what He wants, I won't.

"For where envying and strife is, there is confusion and every evil work" (James 3:16). I could have allowed strife (with my husband) and envy (wanting advancement) to remain motivating me and perpetuating confusion and disobedience. I could have let them keep me from calling on His help. "Call unto me and I will answer you, and show you great and mighty things which you know not" (Jeremiah 33:3). He will show us anything we need to know – but only if we call on Him.

If I had been determined to avoid the time with my husband, I would not have heard the will of God. I would have chosen the letter of the law and decided that the commandment "Thou shalt have no other gods before me" (Exodus 20:3) applied to the situation and I must put God before my husband and go to the meeting.

We must truly want God's voice and ask for His leading and His light before the darkness of confusion can be dispersed from our minds and hearts

If you are confused, ask God for wisdom, knowing that He wants to give you that wisdom. Next make sure that there are no leadings that include a lie about God's nature of love. Then seek scriptural answers to your problem. When His light dawns in your heart, you will not only see the wisdom for your current dilemma but you will see motives which recur in causing confusion in other areas. Those motives can then be submitted to the Lord.

Sometimes the things that cause us confusion can be buried far beneath our consciousness. I remember one day when I wasn't even going to the Lord about a particular situation. In my prayer time, I said, "Lord I know there are lies in my heart. Would you show me one?" Immediately I heard, "You believe that you messed up my plan for your life by your sin."

My first reaction was a stunned silence. Then "Yeeeeeeeeeeees….and the lie is?"

86

Obviously I had messed up His plan for my life by getting pregnant at age 16, going through two failed marriages, as well as other failures and mistakes too numerous to name.

He then said "I sit outside of time and space and see the end from the beginning. I see all choices you ever made or will make. My personal plan for your redemption was based on your sinful choices."

Wow! The Redemption Plan for Amy Barkman was based on every sin she would commit all the days of her life! At every turn, the Redeemer is there waiting to implement His redemption in that situation.

Years of confusion fled at that one sentence "My personal plan for your redemption was based on your sinful choices."

My oldest daughter is one of the greatest joys of my life and a light of God's love wherever she goes. An unspoken confusion inside my heart was that God must have wanted me to commit that sin that resulted in her birth because she is so wonderful to everyone who knows her. I knew that couldn't be true so I had become aware that He was a wonderful Redeemer but wondered what His plan for me was before I messed it up. And if I hadn't messed up, would she have ever been born? Since any plan that didn't include that sin obviously wouldn't have included her existence I really didn't even want to know about it and was glad it didn't happen. But wasn't that sinful – to be glad that God's perfect will had not come to pass? Confusion, failure to distinguish between things, not knowing where one is – all resulted in the belief that somehow the life I live is a second best one.

But now what joy! His plan for me was based on my sinfulness, my weakness, my ignorance, and even my disobedience. What a Redeemer!

HIS REDEMPTION PLAN FOR YOU WAS BASED ON THE SINFUL CHOICES HE KNEW YOU WOULD MAKE.

Sometimes we don't want to know the lies in our hearts. Sometimes we don't want to know His will. But even then, we can call on Him. As that wonderful oldest daughter of mine taught me to pray, "God, I give you permission to change my want to's."

"He restoreth my soul: He leads me in the paths of righteousness for His name's sake" (Psalm 23:3).

When your soul is confused – your mind, will, and emotions all in turmoil – God will lead you into right paths for His name's sake. His name is Jesus – the salvation of Jehovah!

THINGS TO REMEMBER

The Battle Against Confusion

1. God promises to give you wisdom for every situation.

2. The devil will always lie to you about God.

3. You usually have several different motives in your mind and heart.

4. There is an answer in the Bible for your every problem.

5. There is peace on the paths where God leads you.

6. God's redemption plan for your life was based on your sinful choices. You can relax in His Love.

Scripture Truths

"If any of you lack wisdom, let him ask of God, that gives to all men liberally, and upbraids not; and it shall be given him."
James 1:5

"All scripture is given by inspiration of God, and is profitable for doctrine, for reproof, for correction, for instruction in righteousness: that the man of God may be perfect, throughly furnished unto all good works." II Timothy 3:16,17

"For you shall go out with joy, and be led forth with peace..."
Isaiah 55:12

"And your ears shall hear a word behind you, saying 'This is the way, walk in it' when you turn to the right hand, and when you turn to the left."   Isaiah 30:21

FOR THE LORD GOD WILL HELP ME; THEREFORE I SHALL NOT BE CONFOUNDED.   Isaiah 50: 7

Chapter Nine

The Battle Against Enemies

"For we wrestle not against flesh and blood, but against principalities, against powers, against the rulers of the darkness of this world, against spiritual wickedness in high places." Ephesians 6:12

This book is about "**Everyday** Spiritual Warfare" and in it we are not going to delve into areas that are not common to every Christian. This book is not about demon possession or exorcism. We look at the nature of evil spirits only as they affect humans by planting lies in our minds against the Word and Will of God.

Paul writes that we do not wrestle against flesh and blood but against powers of evil in varying offices and ranks in the spiritual realm which we cannot see. I don't know about you but it seems to me that I wrestle against flesh and blood a lot…..my own and that of others. But since Paul wrote that under the direction of God who is Truth, I must accept it, and so must you in order to understand our true enemy.

We have established that God is not the enemy, but we now need to realize that other people and even our own flesh and blood are not our enemies. We have one enemy, one adversary, "Be sober, be vigilant; because your adversary the devil, as a roaring lion, walks about, seeking whom he may devour" (II Peter 5:8). The devil has an army of spirit helpers but he is the instigator of adversity in every form.

I remember the time a few years ago when I began to realize this truth. I was away from home preaching a revival and studying for the evening service when a well-known verse from II Timothy leaped out at me with fresh meaning. "I exhort therefore that first of all supplications, prayers, intercessions, and giving of thanks be made for all men; for kings and for all that are in authority; that we may lead a quiet and peaceable life in all godliness and honesty" (II Tim.2:1,2). I realized that when I was growing up I had heard those in authority prayed for each Sunday morning without fail...and still often hear Christian leaders pray for our government leaders. But I had not, to the best of my knowledge, heard anyone pray for all men. And that was the first exhortation....that supplications, prayers, intercessions, and giving of thanks be made for **all men.**

I read it again...and again. And it gave me a God's eye view of the world.

We are to see ourselves as a part of the entire human race and pray for them, give thanks for them, intercede for them, make requests on their behalf. God sees mankind all in the same category. Jesus died for all mankind (John 3:16). God was in Christ reconciling the entire world to Himself, not holding the sins of anyone against them (II Cor. 5:19).

Our tendency is to see the people in the world who do not believe exactly as we do about God as His enemies and as our enemies. And sometimes we see people – even those who do believe the way we do – acting like enemies to God and to ourselves. But the true enemy behind their actions is the adversary, the devil, who has deceived them into joining the wrong side of the war.

If we can ever get this truth into our hearts and minds, our warfare becomes far more powerful.

Your spouse is not your enemy; your teenager's friends are not your enemy; your boss is not your enemy; the person who gossips about you or rejects you or hurts you is not your enemy. The person who steals from you or kills your loved one or attacks your country is not your enemy. You and these other human beings are in the same category....human beings for whom Jesus died in order to set us free from the true enemy.

Jesus called other humans our "enemies" when they join the forces of adversity but then He told us how to handle them. "You have heard that it has been said 'You shall love your neighbor and hate your enemy' but I say to you love your enemies, bless them that curse you, do good to them that hate you, and pray for them which despitefully use you and persecute you; that you may be the children of your Father which is in heaven; for He makes his sun to rise on the evil and on the good, and sends rain on the just and on the unjust" (Matthew 5:43 – 45).

We are to do good things for the people who hate us. We are to say good things about the people who say bad things about us. We are to pray for (not against) those who do bad things to us. We are to do this because we are made in the image of God.

Jesus said that "every kingdom divided against itself is brought to desolation" (Matthew 12:25). He was talking about Satan and his forces not being divided, on the occasion of Himself being accused of being in league with the devil by healing and casting out demons. But it is a truth about mankind too.

You have heard the maxim "divide and conquer." That is exactly what the devil does to the race of man. He hates us, all of us, because we have authority in the earth that he wants and will never have. So he deceives us into using our authority for his purposes. Some of us are used against others by physically doing damage, some of us are used against others by emotionally doing damage, many of us are used against others by speaking out curses.

Surely that last is only done among the ones who practice witchcraft?

Wrong! Much cursing of others is done by Christians. Cursing is to speak bad things about another.

I have heard many Christians prophesy doom on people. "He will come to a bad end." "She is going to end up ruining herself." "They will never change." "She is no good." "He is worthless."

I have even heard Christians invite doom on people, often people they love. "Whatever you need to do, God, to get them back on the right path, whatever you need to take away from them, however you need to hurt them, do it!" And of course since the true God is the giver of good gifts and the healer, He will do nothing of the kind. But the deceiver, the "god of this world" (II Cor. 4:4) will come in with great glee to "kill, steal, and destroy" (John 10:10) and he will do it on your authority. You will have licensed him to damage the one you care about.

We are told in I John 5:14 that if we ask according to God's will, He hears us and gives us what we desire. We need to ask ourselves, "Who hears and answers us when we ask against God's will?"

"Do you despise the riches of His goodness and forbearance and longsuffering; not knowing that the goodness of God leads you to repentance" (Romans 2:4). Many Christians can answer, "Yes, I have despised the riches of His goodness and patience and have not known that the goodness of God is what leads to repentance."

Why is that? Why do we assume that bad and destructive things have led people to God and so they must have come from God?

Twice this past week I have heard stories about preachers who said they didn't want to be preachers and ran from the call of God. One of them lost his car and his girlfriend and had his arms broken, the other lost a young child in an automobile accident. Both of these preachers attributed these losses to God and said they finally "surrendered to preach the gospel." I assume they agreed to do what they perceived God wanted in order to stop Him from stealing, killing, and destroying in their lives.

But then what gospel, what "good news" do they have to pass on to others? They will pass on the "good news" that God comes to kill, steal, and destroy unless you do exactly what He wants you to do. And that is a lie from hell. It results in the enemy enjoying having his character and actions extolled as god.

Which God do you know? The God of mercy and grace and love who sent Jesus so that "you may have life and have it in abundance" (John 10:10), or the god of this world?

I used to say, "I am not judgmental except toward judgmental people." And I thought I was being not only clever but godly, because after all Jesus got upset with the Pharisees of His day. But then I began to see that judgment of any kind toward others is wrong in me and that God's mercy always rejoices over His justice. I am not to judge so that I will not be judged. I am to be merciful so that I may receive mercy.

Why then is it that sometimes people turn to God when the enemy has done bad things in their lives? Because the enemy is not wise. When a person turns away from God, they turn away from all the blessings He gives; they turn away from His grace and protection. They make themselves vulnerable to the enemy. Then the enemy usually goes too far and the misery he causes brings people to stop running from God. They turn to Him seeking His goodness. And as soon as anyone turns to God, He receives them with open arms.

The preachers who perpetuate the lie that God causes bad things are not my enemy or yours even though they are acting as enemies of Truth and Love. Those preachers are victims of the father of lies. And we need to pray for them, intercede for them, give thanks for them, and make petitions for them until they are free from deception.

A lot of what we label "the enemy" is happening because we have not seen the true enemy and have joined his ranks against other humans. He is "the accuser of the brethren" (Revelation 12:10).

After I got a divorce, there were a lot of people who speculated about me, gossiped about me, lied about me. Some of the things they said were true but many were not true. Ten years later when the Lord was leading me back into the ministry, there was a woman who warned people against me because of my past. I kept having people tell me that she warned them against having anything to do with me. One day I was on the phone with someone telling me about one of those warnings, and it seemed one time too many. Out of my mouth poured the facts of the divorce and what had really gone on and who had really done some things of which I had been accused.

When I got off the phone, instead of feeling better I felt sick at my stomach. The words "ministry of the devil" kept going over and over in my head. And Revelation 12:10 came to my mind, "the accuser of the brethren."

But I hadn't said anything that was not factual!

It didn't matter....I had passed on bad things about others. I got on my knees and asked God to forgive me for spreading those evil reports.

Then He asked me a question. "WHY DID YOU GET SO ANGRY?" I was startled. Surely He knew why.

"Because it wasn't true."

Then He asked another question, just four words but they changed my life. "WHAT IF IT WAS?"

What if I had been guilty of adultery and lying? Well then others would be justified in being suspicious of me. Wouldn't they?

Then I realized that I had been seeing my innocence in that area as justification. I realized that if I were going to be justified by my good deeds then I would have to be condemned for every bad deed that I have done. I realized that nothing matters except grace, that I am justified only by the Blood of Jesus.

I realized – and truly experienced emotionally – that it didn't matter what other people said about me. If it was true or if it was not true had no bearing on my relationship with God or His ability to put me where He wants me in life. His grace is sufficient for me and I can rest in His goodness; any goodness in me is simply His life at work.

And if I am justified only by the Blood of Jesus so is everyone else.

IN OUR FIGHT AGAINST THE REAL ENEMY, WE COME INTO A DEEPER LEVEL OF THE BATTLE AGAINST UNFORGIVENESS.

We often have unforgiveness on a subconscious level. But when we recognize that all men are in the same category in God's eyes – all in need of His grace and mercy, all recipients of lies about God and themselves, we can begin to root out that subconscious bitterness and criticism against those that we have labeled enemies.

God promises, "When a man's ways please the Lord, he makes even his enemies to be at peace with him" (Proverbs 16:17). I have seen it happen.

When I realized that I am justified only by the Blood of Jesus and not my own works, since I realized who the true

Enemy is and truly forgave from my heart the people who spoke against me, things have changed in my life. I am now on friendly terms with people who wouldn't speak to me for years, including the one who warned people against me. And some of those who spoke out are now restored as dear friends.

One of the curses you are redeemed from is, "The Lord shall cause you to "be smitten before your enemies" (Deut. 28:25). No matter who The Enemy uses to act out his adversarial role toward you, God will not let you be destroyed. "You shall hide them in the secret of Your presence from the pride of man: you shall keep them secretly in a pavilion from the strife of tongues" (Psalm 31:20).

And, finally, Paul exhorts us "Dearly beloved, avenge not yourselves...for it is written, Vengeance is mine; I will repay, says the Lord. Therefore if your enemy hungers, feed him; if he thirst, give him drink; for in so doing you shall heap coals of fire on his head. Be not overcome by evil, but overcome evil with good" (Romans 12: 19 – 21).

We look at that promise "you shall heap coals of fire" on the head of our enemy and assume that it is going to make our enemies burn with shame or cause some other discomfort. But when we realize the culture in which that was written, we learn differently.

In the desert culture where dangers lurked for travelers, fire was carried in pots on the head to insure that during each night there would be life-maintaining warmth against the cold. So to heap coals of fire on an enemies' head is to give him or her those things that will mean life to them.

This scripture is telling us that God is the only one who can bring vengeance on the true enemy, the devil. And He will do so in His time.

We are to be kind to those who are acting as enemies, giving them what is necessary for their lives and in so doing, we overcome the lies that the enemy has planted in their hearts and minds, and overcome the evil in them with good.

And we are to pray for them.

THINGS TO REMEMBER

The Battle Against Enemies

1. No human being is your real enemy.

2. Your enemies are the forces of evil.

3. Only God can take vengeance on the devil.

4. You can win people away from the enemy by your good deeds to them.

5. God will cause people who have acted like your enemies to be at peace with you.

Scripture Truths

"For we wrestle not against flesh and blood, but against principalities, against powers, against the rulers of the darkness of this world, against spiritual wickedness in high places."　　　　　　　　　　Ephesians 6:12

"You have heard that it has been said 'You shall love your neighbor and hate your enemy' but I say to you love your enemies, bless them that curse you, do good to them that hate you, and pray for them which despitefully use you and persecute you;"　　　　　　　Matthew 5:43, 44

"Dearly beloved, avenge not yourselves...for it is written, Vengeance is mine; I will repay, says the Lord. Therefore if your enemy hungers, feed him; if he thirst, give him drink; for

in so doing you shall heap coals of fire on his head. Be not overcome by evil, but overcome evil with good."

Romans 12: 19 – 21

"When a man's ways please the Lord, he makes even his enemies to be at peace with him." Proverbs 16:17

NO WEAPON FORMED AGAINST YOU SHALL PROSPER AND EVERY TONGUE THAT RISES AGAINST YOU IN JUDGEMENT YOU SHALL CONDEMN. THIS IS THE HERITAGE OF THE SERVANTS OF THE LORD AND THEIR RIGHTEOUSNESS IS OF ME, SAYS THE LORD.

Isaiah 54:17

Chapter Ten

The Battle Against Accidents

"For he shall give his angels charge over you, to keep you in all your ways."   Psalm 91: 11

My family loves Psalm 91! My Bible is open to it as I sit belted in a plane ready for takeoff. My daughters read it over their children while they are still in the womb. It is on my mind when I am waiting for the dentist. I hand out its verses to people who are afraid of contagious diseases. I think of it when I think of accidents of any kind. Psalm 91 makes it clear that accidents are not from God.

Psalm 91 promises that the person who makes the Lord his or her refuge and fortress, the person who dwells in the secret place of the most High, will live under the protection of the Almighty.

That statement makes some Christians angry or confused because a lot of Christians and their loved ones have accidents, and sometimes they are fatal accidents.

Am I saying that people who have accidents are not good Christians? Absolutely not. I have had accidents and my family has had accidents.

But we are redeemed from them, nevertheless. Accidents are never God's will.

"As the bird by wandering, as the swallow by flying, the curse causeless shall not come" (Proverbs 26:2).

If something bad happens to you or me or our loved ones, there is a reason for it; it has to get there by some motivating power. And we have established that the enemy is the devil; he is the one who is motivated toward the destruction of mankind.

Are we then at the mercy of the devil and whatever accident he wants to send our way? Must we live in terror that our spouse, children, parents, friends may be suddenly devastated by the whim of the enemy?

NO!

We have promises from God concerning the whims, schemes, and desires of the enemy.

"The wicked shall see it and be grieved; he shall gnash with his teeth, and melt away; the desire of the wicked shall perish" (Psalms 112:10).

What causes this anguish on the part of the devil that is recorded in Psalm 112?

What is the secret of the defeat of his desire? The writer has described the cause earlier in the psalm. "Blessed is the man that feareth the Lord...He shall not be afraid of evil tidings; his heart is fixed, trusting in the Lord" (verses 1 and 7). This entire Psalm is a description of the life of a man who fears the Lord.

Most of us fear what the devil or other men can do to us instead of getting our priorities in order and seeing the Lord God as the most important force to be reckoned with in our experience. When we revere Him and stand in awe of Him, everything else in life falls into place. We see that He is more powerful than any other force in the Universe.

Doesn't this mean that whatever happens to those who have put Him first, those who "fear him", must be His will?

And if not, why doesn't He take care of everyone all the time, especially Christians?

GOD ORDAINED THAT MAN IS IN AUTHORITY IN THE EARTH AND EVERYTHING THAT IS RECEIVED FROM HIM COMES FROM FAITH IN HIS WORD.

God and His Word are one. If you do not trust His Word, you are not trusting in Him. And He only does what is promised and received by faith.

"The Lord is my light and my salvation; whom shall I fear? The Lord is the strength of my life; of whom shall I be afraid? When the wicked, even my enemies and my foes came upon me to eat up my flesh, they stumbled and fell. Though a host should encamp against me, my heart shall not fear; though war should rise against me, in this will I be confident" (Psalm 27: 1-3).

Is your confidence in the Lord that settled? Does your faith in His promises of good things outweigh fear of what the devil or people or bad circumstances can do to you? Is your heart fixed, trusting in the Lord?

Unfortunately, most of our hearts are not fixed; we are not trusting in the Lord to fulfill His promises to protect us and our loved ones. Our hearts are not fixed - because of the pollution of the good news about God's nature that has crept into the Church.

The wrong "sovereignty of God" concept has caused God to be blamed for much that the devil causes. As we said earlier in looking at the principles of spiritual warfare, we will not fight against what we believe to be the will of God.

An accident according to the New World Dictionary is "an unpleasant and unintended happening, sometimes resulting from negligence, that results in injury, loss, damage, etc."

"Injury, loss, damage" – sounds like it proceeds from the one who "comes to steal, kill, and destroy" (John 10:10), doesn't it?

Accidents are not from God. They are unpleasant, they kill, steal, and destroy. They are not intended by God or man, but by the enemy of God and man; they are part of the chaos that resulted as part of the fall away from connectedness with God.

Since we can't see accidents coming, how can we prevent them?

We can't. But the Word can.

That is why Psalm 91 is a favorite of my family. The promises in it are the Sword of the Spirit that my family uses to protect ourselves from the chaos of accidents. Belief in those promises are the armor we stand in so that, "A thousand shall fall at your side and ten thousand at your right hand; but it shall not come near you" (Psalm 91:7).

Does God love my family more than other families? Not at all!!! But my family has fixed their hearts in the promises of protection from accidents. Do we want those at our side and at our right hand to fall? Definitely not!!! But we also know that it will not help those who are falling for us to fall also.

We know that we are redeemed from this curse of the law: "And your life shall hang in doubt before you; and you shall fear day and night, and shall have no assurance of your life" (Deuteronomy 28:66).

We believe that the Lord promises, "With long life will I satisfy him, and show him my salvation" (Psalm 91:16).

This is not presumption on our parts; we believe that the Lord gave those promises because He wants all human beings to believe and appropriate them. "Whereby are given to us exceeding great and precious promises: that by these you might be partakers of the divine nature, having escaped the corruption that is in the world through lust" (II Peter 1:4).

God gave us promises and wants us to "partake" of them. He "prepares a table before us in the presence of our enemies" (Psalm 23:5). That table is not in heaven – there are no enemies there. That table of abundant life promises is here and now in the midst of all the accidents and destruction designed by the enemy.

God has prepared a feast of promises for us to partake of, to dine on, to live by, to walk in. They are for whosoever will come and receive them.

"Partake", according to the New World Dictionary is "to take a portion; to eat or drink something". No wonder Job could say "I have esteemed the words of His mouth more than my necessary food" (Job 23:12).

That faith in God's Word of promise is how God was able to redeem all the terrible accidents that happened in Job's life and why God could say that Job had, "spoken of me the thing that is right" (Job 42:8). Because of this trust in the faithfulness of God, "the Lord blessed the later end of Job more than his beginning" (Job 42:12).

Job lived and had a relationship with God long before the Savior came to show us the true nature of God, even long before Isaiah wrote that the Savior would be "wounded for our transgressions, bruised for our iniquities" (Isaiah 54:5).

Surely we who have been shown that Jesus bore our sins and their effects can learn to trust the goodness of God and His promises of protection.

I think one of the most horrible lies ever told about God is that "He was lonesome for that child and called them back to heaven." God is never lonesome for any of us unless we have turned our back on companionship with Him, and even then He will not end our lives to "be with us." He is here with us at all times. In Him we live and move and have our being.

That lie about His character and actions is one by which the devil has stolen children from Christian parents. If we don't know that God promises humans at least 70 years (Psalm 90:10), we will be vulnerable to fear of the future; our lives, and the lives of our loved ones, "will hang in doubt before us."

My husband served in Viet Nam for two tours of duty. He said the mentality was that there was a big computer in the sky that randomly chose times of death. If your number came up, you would die. If it didn't, you would live.

Many people believe that there is an appointed time to die. They get that from the passage in Ecclesiastes which says, "To everything there is a season, and a time to every purpose under the heaven: A time to be born, and a time to die" (Ecclesiastes 3:1,2). But the scripture goes on to say that there is "a time to weep, and a time to laugh...a time to mourn, and a time to dance...a time to embrace, and a time to refrain from embracing...a time to keep silence and a time to speak" (vs. 4-7). We would think a person was foolish if, in the midst of a time of great fun and fellowship, they looked at their watch and said "Uh-Oh...it's time to weep," and then began crying in the midst of everyone else's laughter. There is not a set time for us to embrace or speak or dance or laugh ...or die.

The word time, "eth" in Hebrew, can mean an appointed time but we can see from the context that is not what is meant in this passage. "Eth" also means "proper or appropriate" time, and "season". In the passage where birth and death are coupled with mourning and dancing, weeping and laughing, speaking and silence, it is obvious that the second or third definition of the word is meant. There is an appropriate time for everything under the sun; there is a season for these things.

One of the benefits listed in Psalm 103 is "He redeems my life from destruction" (verse 4). That Hebrew word shachath is translated "pit" instead of "destruction" in several versions and the Hebrew dictionary says that the connotation of "pit" means a trap. One of the benefits of God to you is redemption from the destructive traps of the devil, the accidents he plans in order to steal or kill or destroy in your life.

I remember one time, shortly after I had heard about the protection promised in Psalm 91, I was driving home from work on a very icy road. I lost control of the car and it went skating over the ice toward a 20 foot drop off on the side of the road. Neither the brakes nor the steering wheel had any effect on the course of the car toward that drop off.

I knew that disaster was imminent but I had been studying Psalm 91 and knew it could be avoided. I believed that if I could speak a protection promise out loud, I would be safe. But I couldn't think of any words; I remembered the concept but all words escaped me. As I saw the edge of the shoulder coming closer I just said out loud a negative "Uh uh!" meaning "No - this can't happen." My mind denied the right of that accident to come to pass and when that denial came out of my mouth, without a touch of my foot to the brake or any other visible cause, my car came to a complete stop. I backed away from the edge and traveled home without further incident.

I remember the day that one of my daughters was told that a prenatal test did not look good and she should consider having another test and possibly an abortion. The first words out of my mouth were, "Our hearts are fixed, trusting in the Lord," and my daughter told the doctors that she wouldn't have an abortion anyway so there was no sense in having the other test. Several months later she gave birth to a very healthy little boy who at age seven accepted Jesus as Savior and was baptized.

Some would say that there was no cause and effect in the course of that pregnancy. And maybe they are right. It may be that there was never anything wrong with the baby. All I know is that time after time over the years we have had opportunities to be afraid of bad things happening but we rejected them in favor of trusting that God is good all the time and that all good things come from God. And time after time we have been proven right.

It's all about faith. It's all about what you believe and Who you believe.

Jesus said, "Whosoever shall say....and shall not doubt in his heart, but shall believe that those things which he says shall come to pass; he shall have whatsoever he says" (Mark 11:23).

Many Christians have faith in God for the afterlife but comparatively few are trusting Him for all He wants to give here and now.

What are you saying?

Are you saying, "I'm afraid that I will get the flu, have a wreck, lose my family, fall down, have my purse stolen...?"

Or are you saying "He gives His angels guard over me to protect me in all my ways."

You are to speak out your faith in God's promises. That is the praise that causes the enemy to "fall back and perish at His presence" (Psalm 9:3).

"For I know the thoughts that I think toward you, says the Lord, thoughts of peace, and not of evil, to give you an expected end" (Jeremiah 29:11).

This particular concept has confused a lot of people who have quoted protection scriptures and still have had accidents. But each of us must ask ourselves if we are quoting those scriptures because we are afraid of accidents and trying to use scripture like some kind of magic to ward them off, or is our heart truly fixed on trust in the promises of God and speaking out the scriptures as a sword against the enemy who comes to kill, steal, and destroy.

God does not throw unexpected bad things at you.

God has invested His sovereignty in His Word to be received by faith by whosoever will receive His Word and exercise Truth in their circumstances.

THINGS TO REMEMBER

The Battle Against Accidents

1. Accidents are not from God but are a part of chaos.

2. God's sovereignty rests in His Word through man's lips.

3. The word of God promises protection from accidents.

4. Believing and speaking out faith in God's promises provides a shield of protection from accidents.

Scripture Truths

"For he shall give his angels charge over you, to keep you in all your ways."   Ps. 91: 11

"The Lord is my light and my salvation; whom shall I fear? The Lord is the strength of my life; of whom shall I be afraid? When the wicked, even my enemies and my foes came upon me to eat up my flesh, they stumbled and fell. Though a host should encamp against me, my heart shall not fear; though war should rise against me, in this will I be confident."

Psalm 27: 1-3

"With long life will I satisfy him, and show him my salvation."   Psalm 91:16

"Be sober, be vigilant; because your adversary the devil, as a roaring lion, walks about, seeking whom he may devour; whom resist steadfast in the faith..." I Peter 5:8,9

LET THE REDEEMED OF THE LORD SAY SO, WHOM HE HAS REDEEMED FROM THE HAND OF THE ENEMY. Psalm 107: 2

Chapter Eleven

The Battle Against Poverty

"And God is able to make all grace abound toward you; that you, always having all sufficiency in all things, may abound to every good work."

II Corinthians 9:8

The New World Dictionary defines poverty as "the condition of being poor; deficiency in necessary properties or desirable qualities; inadequacy; smallness in amount".

We are going to define poverty as a deficiency of material goods or money.

Even though most of the Western world is rich in comparison with the vast majority of the world's population, we often feel that we are deficient in what we see as necessities of life in our modern culture. We make jokes about having days left over at the end of our paychecks. We sometimes feel that there is smallness in the amount we are paid contrasted to what we see others are paid.

This chapter is about the battle against lack of possessions or finances. First of all, according to Galatians 3:13 you are redeemed from the curse of the law which says in Deuteronomy 28:17 that "Cursed shall be your basket and your store." That would translate to your purse and your bank account. But the blessing to which you are redeemed is that "Blessed shall be your basket and your store." And "The Lord shall command the blessing upon you in your storehouses, and in all that you set your hand to…" (Deuteronomy 28:5, 8).

If you are in Christ Jesus, you are redeemed from lack of any kind. We are told in Galatians that we are redeemed from the curse that comes from not following God's law so that we can walk in the blessings of Abraham.

Those blessing are given in Deuteronomy 28:2-28, but we can also see in Genesis, from the mouth of Abraham's servant, how some of those blessings manifested to him in practical ways. The servant was sent to Abraham's family in the land of his youth to find a wife for his son Isaac. The servant gave this report of his master. "The Lord has blessed my master greatly; and he is become great: and he has given him flocks, and herds, and silver, and gold, and menservants, and maidservants, and camels, and asses" (Genesis 24:35).

The same blessings that the Lord blessed Abraham with are promised to you and me in Christ Jesus. I personally don't want flocks and herds in my back yard and you may not either but those things represent businesses or careers that bring prosperity to us. I have no desire for a camel or a donkey and you probably don't either; but we very much want good reliable transportation. We want sufficient money and adequate helpers for whatever we need to accomplish. All these things are blessings that God gives to the ones "who are of faith blessed with faithful Abraham" (Galatians 3:9).

The enemy who comes to steal, kill, and destroy (John 10:10) comes to take your blessings of prosperity as well as steal your peace, joy, and love. Poverty in any degree is part of chaos, a symptom of the absence of Shalom, a result of not being completely connected with God. In fact the Hebrew word Shalom - wholeness, completeness - is often translated "prosperity."

I opened this chapter with a quote from the ninth chapter of II Corinthians. The entire eighth and ninth chapters of that letter are about financial resources. Paul is addressing the church on the subject of giving and receiving physical provision. He makes the statement to them "For you know the grace of our Lord Jesus Christ, that though he was rich, yet for your sakes he became poor, that you through his poverty might be rich" (II Cor. 8:9). It is by grace that we become rich. Grace is undeserved favor, unearned blessings... and we need to keep that in mind. God's prosperity is poured out on us by grace, not because of anything we do to earn it.

In Chapter 9 of II Corinthians, we read that "Every man according as he purposes in his heart, so let him give, not grudgingly, or of necessity, for God loves a cheerful giver. And God is able to make all grace abound toward you; that you always having all sufficiency in all things, may abound to every good work" (verses 7 and 8).

The grace that abounds toward you so that you will always have all sufficiency in all things is the grace mentioned earlier in the previous chapter, that grace of our Lord Jesus Christ who became poor so that you could become rich.

But the passage says it is when we give cheerfully that God can make that grace abound toward us.

???

Doesn't that put a condition on grace and make it not grace at all but something deserved?

No.

Cheerful giving is an attitude of the heart that is filled with faith knowing that God is the Provider at all times.

The verse says that to give cheerfully is to give "not grudgingly or of necessity". Giving "of necessity" would include giving to get a return. When we give out of fear or duty to God, buying His provision by some act, whether it is a tenth of our income or one dollar a week put in the collection plate, our hearts are not trusting in His grace. When we give grudgingly or out of duty to mankind, we are seeing ourselves as their provider instead of as a mere instrument of the Lord's provision.

The Lord wants us to see material provision as coming from Him and flowing out whenever and wherever it is needed. I remember once having a vision of the Lord holding a bag of gold and pouring it out to my husband and me. The purse was small but the heap of gold coins that came from it was as tall as my waist the last time I looked at it as He poured. For years I kept looking for the huge amount of money heaped up and finally I realized what the vision meant. "… provide <u>yourselves bags which do not grow old, a treasure in the heavens</u> that do not fail, where no thief comes, nor moth corrupts" (Luke 12:33). Our provision from Him is a continuing steady flow.

Both my husband and I love to give to others. It is that attitude of cheerful giving, and trusting that our needs will be met by Him, that allows God to continually pour out to us not only necessities but many luxuries.

We don't have a budget. My husband laughs and says that we wouldn't dare make a budget. Our regular income is very small and it would scare us to look at a list of our income and needs. That fear would pollute our faith. But by just trusting His provision, we have everything we need and more luxuries than most people.

How does it happen? It's that treasure in the heavens that the Lord pours out upon us continually; we don't analyze it; we just receive it.

That lifestyle would be difficult for most people, and not all people are called to it; but it is the way we are all called to live in attitude if not in actual practice. My husband and I have spent most of our lives with no savings accounts or investments but many other people are called to have those things. It is when their trust is in those accounts and investments instead of in the Lord that the problems arise and the thief comes to steal.

In the Lord's prayer which most of the Body of Christ prays on a regular basis, we say "Give us this day our daily bread" (Matt. 6:11). But most of us do not really mean it. We really mean "Give me this day enough bread for a year or more....so I can see it and touch it and not have to worry or depend on You continually." I know because I lived that way for decades!

God's provision is unconditional. To hear some preachers, you would think that His provision is granted only to those who tithe or those who are big givers into the kingdom. But that's not how God works or who He is. Jesus taught us to pray for God to give us our daily bread...no strings attached. The only provisional petition in the Lord's Prayer is forgiveness: "Forgive us our debts as we forgive our debtors" (Matt. 6:12). He did not say that we are to pray "Give us this day our daily bread as we give our money to You and/or others."

God pours out Himself in provision to His creation. The Word tells us that "God is love" (I John 4:8). The word "love" is the Greek "agape" and literally means "a love feast". Jesus said "I am the living bread which came down from heaven" (John 6:51). When we partake of the elements of the Lord's supper, we are receiving Him, but that means of grace should also serve to remind us that every good thing we receive as sustenance is from Him, His Word made flesh, Himself poured out for us.

In Roman mythology there is a story of Jupiter disguising himself as a shower of gold and pouring himself through a window to make himself acceptable to a woman to whom he was attracted. That is nonsense; BUT.... as in many of these myths, the story has within it a grain of truth.

117

God, the one true God, Jehovah Jireh, the Lord Your Provider, is one with His Word of provision and that Word does become flesh wherever it is received.

I was appointed as pastor of a church 40 miles from my home and so obviously cannot walk each time I need to be there. God promised to provide my transportation needs and I trusted Him for that even though my vehicle appeared to be on its last legs...or axles ☺. I didn't even pray about it as a petition; I simply told the Lord I knew He would get me where He had called me to be and thanked Him for being my provider.

I didn't care how He did it. He could keep my current vehicle running, He could have someone take me in their car, or He could give me another car. I really didn't care one way or another, but I had no money for repairs or new cars.

There is something freeing about not being able to meet your own needs; you are delivered from scheming and planning because there is nothing to scheme and plan with, nothing you can do about the situation. You have no choice but to trust the Lord.

Shortly after thanking Him for meeting my needs, I received a phone call from a lady who said that she was out driving and saw a 3 year old van for sale and the Holy Spirit said to her "That van is Amy's. Buy it for her." And she did.

God caused His Word concerning meeting my transportation needs to become flesh in the material of that van. Whenever I drove that van, I was aware of Himself being my provision of transportation. And continue being aware of Jehovah Jireh in my new car.

I believe the key to receiving provision from the Lord is dependence on Him as Provider. If we are looking to jobs or people or governments to provide for us, we can't give cheerfully because we see a limited amount of money... and if we give it away, it's that much less that we have. But if our provision is dependent on the One who creates all resources, there is no limit to what can flow to and through us.

Do not think that I am speaking against large salaries or savings accounts or investments. I am not. I often pray with people for salary increases and for their "storehouses" to be full. And I often benefit from people the Lord has blessed with large incomes.

A good friend of mine who has come to expect God to deal with her through dreams had a dream one night about a certain stock; at the time the stock was paying twenty some dollars per share. In the dream she heard "This stock is going to $130 per share."

She invested the money she had, and some other money that she had the oversight of for some young relatives. The stock went to $130 per share and she sold it, making a large profit for herself and her family. At the time of this writing, the stock is at $4 per share.

"I am the Lord thy God which teaches you to profit, which leads you by the way that you should go" (Isaiah 48:17).

We must never put God in a box or expect Him to do things all the time or with all people the way He has done things with us at one time or another. We each need to follow His lead minute by minute and day by day.

THE KEY TO FINANCIAL PEACE IS TO SEE HIM AS PROVIDER AND WALK IN OBEDIENCE.

One day my husband, Gary, said to me with a rueful laugh, "I am going to stop taking any cash with me to church." When I asked why, he said "Every Sunday morning for the last few weeks the Lord has told me to put all my money in the offering plate." We are not talking huge amounts of money but for my husband it was huge – his coffee money and spending money for the week.

He was obedient, but didn't understand why this was asked of him until a few days following his teasing comment to me. An envelope arrived in the mail from someone he had met only on three occasions and had not seen for many years. It contained a check for $3,000 and said that it was money that a man who died years earlier had wanted him to have.

What a surprise!

And my husband immediately said "Now I know why God had me give that money."

Why did God ask Gary to give everything he had on those three occasions? I can think of two possibilities. First it could be that He wanted Gary to know that the money was not just something that happened but was a blessing that God planned. Second, it could have been that Gary giving the money in obedience was a form of spiritual warfare which allowed God's will concerning the money to be carried out through the mind and will of the person who sent it. We don't know why God asked it…but we do know He has a good reason for everything He does.

Wasn't Gary giving "grudgingly or of necessity"? No, even though he joked with me about it, my husband has found over the years that if God asks him to give something, it is because God has a wonderful gift planned to give to him. He gave it cheerfully in obedience to the prompting of the Holy Spirit, knowing that The Provider would meet his own need. And Gary did not go without coffee those three weeks either.

I hope you don't think that I am speaking against tithing either; I am not. But I do hope you realize that a tithe or tenth is a man instigated rule, not something God imposed from the beginning.

The tithe is first mentioned in the fourteenth chapter of Genesis when Abraham was met on his return from a victory by Melchizedik, the Priest of the most High God. Melchizadek blessed Abraham with bread and wine and with words. And Abraham gave him a tenth of all he had won in the battle.

Abraham, a man created in God's image and given authority in the earth, instigated the tithe. God received that tenth of the blessings Abraham had been given and He received that amount as a standard for what man would give back to God as His rightful portion. The tithe became part of the covenant relationship between God and Abraham.

Tithing was part of the interaction between God and the descendants of Abraham that we know as the Old Covenant. Tithing is not mentioned as a part of the New Covenant between the Father and Son. There is no percentage involved in that Covenant; each party gives one hundred percent. But the promises to the tither under the Old Covenant are still valid because of the blessings of Abraham that are ours in Christ Jesus.

"Bring all the tithes into the storehouse, that there may be meat in my house and prove me now, says the Lord of hosts, if I will not open you the windows of heaven and pour you out a blessing that there shall not be room enough to receive it. And I will rebuke the devourer for your sakes...." (Malachi 3:10,11).

Many Christians have waged spiritual warfare against "the devourer" by tithing.

Many Christians have waged spiritual warfare against the enemy by believing God for the "hundredfold return" based on Jesus' statement in Mark 10:29,30. "There is no man that has left house or brothers or sisters or father or mother or wife or children or lands for my sake and the gospel but he shall receive a hundredfold now in this time...."

Some other Christians don't believe that Jesus meant this literally and criticize those who pray for that return on their giving. And if someone is giving just to get that return, they may need to rethink their motives. But I have seen it happen and have heard many stories of it happening. What we have to keep in mind is that it is by faith that we receive from God. If we believe that He will do it because of a promise or principle in His Word, He will.

One of my favorite stories of an hundredfold return happened to my husband before I knew him. He had been impressed to give a certain amount at an evangelistic meeting and he did it. Several weeks later he was bidding on a house at auction and had determined the upper extent that he would pay for the house. He got the house for much less than what he expected to pay and several days later when he figured the difference between what he paid and the amount he expected to pay, it was exactly one hundred times the amount he had been led to give weeks earlier at the meeting.

God loves to give to us. And my personal belief is that a hundredfold is just a fraction of what He wants to give. The One who received five loaves and two fishes and gave back enough to feed more than 5,000 thinks nothing of multiplying by more than 100.

I absolutely love to watch God work in the area of finances. And for me He always provides before a deadline. I have heard a lot of people say that God is an 11th hour God, coming through at the last minute. But I have not experienced that, because I don't believe that He withholds for any period of time. He is the great I AM, not I WILL BE. He is always pouring out to us; we receive when we believe we will receive.

God still works material miracles. One time when I had fried chicken, mashed potatoes, and four ears of corn to feed my family of seven, I thought everything would go round all right except the corn. We all loved creamed corn and a half an ear apiece would not satisfy but it would give each of us a taste. Just as we were setting the table, we were surprised by a family of six who dropped in to visit. I offered for them to join us for dinner, sure that they would decline. But they surprised me and accepted!

As I poured the corn into a bowl I breathed a half joking prayer "Lord, please multiply this food." I knew the Lord would make what we had enough...but I honestly didn't expect the abundance He provided.

I don't know exactly how it happened but I do know that all thirteen people had corn, I had two helpings and there was a little left over. He is a miracle working God. He is the Lord your provider.

He delights in pouring out provision to you.

If He delights and we want....what is our problem? Where is the battle?

The battle, like all battles, is in your mind. If you believe that God does not want you to have something, you will not be able to receive it. "Whatever things you desire, when you pray <u>believe you receive them</u> and you will have them" (Mark 11:24).

THE BATTLE IS TO DISPEL THE LIE THAT GOD IS WITHHOLDING FROM YOU. IT'S THE OLDEST LIE IN THE BOOK.

"Now the serpent was more crafty than any beast of the field which the Lord God had made. And he said to the woman 'Has God said you shall not eat of all the trees of the garden?"(Gen. 3:1). Can you see what he was doing? He was attempting to plant a concept of a stingy God who didn't want mankind to enjoy all the good things around them. When he couldn't make them believe that God really hadn't given them so much to enjoy, he went another route. He didn't really change the lie about God's nature, he just tempered it to the one thing God had told them not to do and painted a picture of God wanting to withhold that because it was a good thing that He wanted to keep all to Himself. The truth, of course, was that it was something that would cause them harm and His command not to partake of it was much like you telling your child not to drink gasoline.

The same God who gave mankind all things to enjoy except the things that became polluted, has made His will concerning our provision known throughout His Word. "He that spared not his own son, but delivered him up for us all, how shall he not with him also freely give us all things?" (Romans 8:32).

Your part of the battle against poverty on any level is to fill your mind with the promises of God concerning His provision, and be obedient to the promptings of the Holy Spirit.

One time when I had almost no money I wanted some placemats for my dining room table. I didn't want plastic mats but something that would look nice there at that end of my living room. I didn't see anything I liked that I could afford but I asked the Lord to provide some for me. One afternoon I went out on an errand and a strong impulse came to me to go to a certain store. I determined that it was the Holy Spirit and went to the store. When I walked in I saw a sale table and on the table were some delicately woven placemats in just the right color....for twenty five cents each!

That may not seem like a big deal to you but it was to me. And the placemats were the forerunner of my van! I didn't give to get either of them. I trusted the Giver.

There are a lot of Christians who believe that it is wrong to want a lot of money. I used to be one of them. But I am learning.

If God wants me to help others, if He wants me to give to the poor, then I need something to help with, something to give. He wants to pour out a blessing so much that I can't contain it. Why? So that He can bless me, and others through me.

We need to learn to receive from Him to demonstrate and be part of His generosity to the world.

God's enemy has always hated that generosity of God's and will do anything he can to stop us from believing in and receiving it.

God wants to pour out an abundance of financial blessings to you so that you can bless others. He wants you to be a part of His generosity system. BELIEVE IT!

THINGS TO REMEMBER

The Battle Against Poverty

1. God loves to bless you with material things, and has made promises to do so.

2. You are redeemed from lack of any kind through Jesus Christ.

3. When you are a cheerful giver, God can pour out great abundance to and through you.

4. You will receive exactly what you believe God wants to give you.

5. The enemy does not want you to be a part of God's generosity system.

Scripture Truths

"Every man according as he purposes in his heart, so let him give, not grudgingly, or of necessity, for God loves a cheerful giver. And God is able to make all grace abound toward you; that you always having all sufficiency in all things may abound to every good work." II Cor. 9:7,8

"He that spared not His own son, but delivered him up for us all, how shall he not with him also freely give us all things?" Romans 8:3

"Bring all the tithes into the storehouse, that there may be meat in my house and prove me now, says the Lord of hosts, if I will not open you the windows of heaven and pour you out a blessing that there shall not be room enough to receive it. And I will rebuke the devourer for your sake..." Malachi 3:10,11

FEAR NOT, LITTLE FLOCK, FOR IT IS YOUR FATHER'S GOOD PLEASURE TO GIVE YOU THE KINGDOM. Luke 12:32

Chapter Twelve

The Battle Against Sickness

*"Bless the Lord, O my soul, and forget not all his
benefits...who heals all your diseases."*
Psalm 103:2,3

Early in the history of the interaction between God
and His Covenant people, He revealed Himself to them as
Healer. It was on the occasion of the deliverance from
Egypt. The pursuing Egyptian army had just been
drowned in the Red Sea, Miriam had led the women in a
song and dance of praise, and all Israel was excited about
God and His care for them.

Then they came to a place called Marah and found that
the waters were undrinkable. These people, who had just
seen mighty acts of God through their leader Moses,
began to murmur against him. Moses cried out to the Lord
and God showed him a tree. When Moses cast the tree into
the water, the waters were made sweet. And God spoke
to the people, "If you will diligently hearken to the voice
of the Lord your God and will do what is right in his sight
and will give ear to his commandments and keep all his
statutes, I will put none of the diseases upon you which I
have brought upon the Egyptians; for I am the Lord that
heals you" (Exodus 15:26).

"I AM JEHOVAH RAPHA" - THE LORD YOUR HEALER.

But is He always? Isn't this revelation of His healing nature dependent on you diligently listening to His voice and doing what is right and obeying all His commandments?

And what about the phrase that concerned the Egyptians..."the diseases which I have brought upon the Egyptians?" Is God the source of disease? Doesn't this imply that He is the one bringing disease on people?

How do we know when God is causing disease and when He wants to heal disease?

You cannot successfully fight what you believe is God's will so it is very important for you to clarify in your mind what you believe about God's will concerning your healing.

Why can you not successfully fight what you believe is God's will?

Because faith is "the substance of things hoped for" (Hebrews 11:1). Faith is trust that the Word of God, which is His will revealed, will come to pass in your life. And that trust is the agency of success in any area. If you don't believe God's promise, you are lacking the thing that makes it happen. If you believe that a bad thing is God's will, you don't have the only agency of power to fight the bad thing.

One time I had been told that if I would read Matthew, Mark, Luke, John, and Acts three times apiece in thirty days, I would get a greater revelation of Jesus. So I did it. That meant reading Matthew through Acts in ten days, three times in a row. The way my Bible is laid out it meant reading approximately eighteen and a half pages a day. It works out to almost twelve chapters daily. I decided to do it.

129

It was a chore. Sometimes I felt almost guilty because I would be reading without comprehension, as a duty, not savoring the Word of God at all. It was much like eating your food on the run, just for energy. And that is exactly what I was doing without realizing it!

It was on the third time through, in the 14th chapter of John, that I got it.

Phillip asked Jesus to show them the Father and Jesus said "Have I been with you so long and yet you have not known me, Phillip? He that has seen me has seen the Father. Why are you saying 'Show me the Father.' Don't you believe that I am in the Father and the Father in me? The words that I speak to you I do not speak of myself; but the Father that lives in me, He does the works" (John 14:9,10).

I laid my Bible down in stunned realization. It was as though Jesus had said "Amy, why do you say 'Show me the will of God?' If you have seen me, you see the will of God in action."

And I realized that through every action of Jesus recorded in the gospels, through every action of the early church acting in His Name and empowered by the same Holy Spirit that empowered Him, I saw healing.

Never once did Jesus say, "I can't heal you because God wants you to stay sick." He never said, "Go away and come back later when you have learned the lesson you are supposed to learn out of this." He never said "God will get lots of glory through your brave suffering." Not once!

In that moment, it was settled for me forever, that it is God's will for healing to happen for all mankind.

The only times Jesus did not heal with great miraculous power was because of the unbelief of the people (Matthew 13:58). I believe with all my heart that Hebrews 13:8 is true and "Jesus Christ is the same yesterday, and today, and forever." The reason we do not receive His healing power in our day and age is because of unbelief.

An unwavering belief in God's desire to always heal everyone makes some people angry. They feel like their faith is being belittled if they have not received healing. But I do not say to anyone else what I do not say to myself. I have received many great healing miracles, but there are areas of healing I have not yet received. It is not God's fault; it is fear and unbelief in my heart that keeps me from believing that I receive and thus having the things I pray for (Mark 11:24).

I think that Jesus Himself marvels at our unbelief just as He did when He walked the earth in Biblical times (Mark 6:6). Even when I received the revelation that God's will for healing and health for the body was revealed in Jesus Christ, I still had to deal with those Old Testament scriptures where God struck people with sickness and disease and brought calamity on them. This was not the God I knew, the God who was revealed to me through Jesus Christ. But I believe that the Word of God is just that....His Word given to us to understand Him, so there must be an answer to these passages.

The very name and designation "Jesus Christ" means "The anointing of the Salvation of God" or "The Anointed One to bring about God's Salvation". Salvation means, in the original Hebrew and Greek – both Old and New Covenants- "deliverance from all temporal evil," and this deliverance includes freedom from sickness and lack.

The original covenant people, Israel, knew that God wanted to heal them. It was a matter of what they needed to do to receive that healing. With them it was to obey the law or make sacrifices to cover their disobedience from the eyes of God. But to us, the New Covenant people, it is to have faith in the accomplished work on Calvary, the sacrifice made once and for all time, and to believe in the grace available to us because of that sacrifice.

But...

But what about those Old Testament passages like "And the anger of the Lord was kindled against Uzzah; and God smote him there for his error and there he died by the ark of God" (II Samuel 6:7). Uzzah did not obey the law to not touch the ark of the Lord. But his heart was in the right place – he was only trying to protect the ark! Why would God be angry toward this man for trying to steady the ark because the oxen that were carrying it shook it and it looked as if it were about to fall?

This and similar passages bothered me...a lot! And I begged the Lord to resolve them for me, to show me their meaning in the light of a God who loves mankind and always wants good for them.

Light and darkness began to separate in my mind concerning this, as well as other bad things that happen to man in the earth, one day as I was reading in Isaiah 14: 11-19 concerning the fall of Lucifer.

This great being decided to use the creative ability conferred on him (he is called the Anointed Cherub in Ezekiel 28:14) to make himself separate from and above God. We are told that he, who had watched God create everything by speaking words, said in his heart "I will ascend into heaven, I will exalt my throne above the stars of God: I will sit also upon the mount of the congregation in the sides of the north. I will ascend above the heights of the clouds; I will be like the most High" (Isaiah 14:13,14). He fully expected his words to come to pass.

Where was this being speaking from that he was going to ascend to heaven? I believe he was speaking from the original garden of God in the earth (Ezekiel 28:13 – 19). He wanted to expand the territory which had been given to him; he wanted to be more important than God, but when he spoke those words, God responded with HIS Word, the source of all creative power and said "You will be brought down to hell, to the sides of the pit" (Isaiah 14:15).

Then God went on to say "Prepare slaughter for his children, for the iniquity of their fathers; that they do not rise, nor possess the land, nor fill the face of the world with cities" (Isaiah 14:21).

There, in those words spoken out against Lucifer who became Satan, lies the answer to the mystery of how God who IS Life can be the author of sickness and death. It was a judgment of God separating Himself from all who would not stay one with His nature. Notice, it is not a personal judgment to individuals. It is a judgment on any being who follows the original rebel into rebellion. Jesus spoke to the Pharisees millennia later saying, "You are of your father, the devil" (John 8:44).

Some of the angels followed Lucifer into rebellion and chaos. Later, mankind followed Lucifer into rebellion and chaos. The devil wanted the separation that was his eternal state to happen to every creature of God's; he wanted his misery to be shared by all creation.

There was no plan of salvation for the spirit beings that changed their nature, the fallen angels. But there was a plan for the salvation of human souls, to restore them to oneness with the spiritual nature of God. "He was brought as a lamb to the slaughter" (Isaiah 53:7), taking on Himself for the whole race of rebellious mankind, the slaughter for the children of rebellion spoken out before the creation of humans.

And there was a plan of salvation for the physical earth and the animals through redeemed mankind (Romans 8:18 – 22).

What God warned mankind against in the Garden of Eden was to not take into themselves a polluted nature, the nature of being one with both good and evil. But they did it anyway. And because the nature that God set in motion in the physical realm was that like begets like, that any living thing will bring forth after its own kind, all mankind has been polluted in nature from that time of pollution.

The death that was lodged in the souls of our first parents was a separation from the wisdom of God; they would see and experience good and evil alike and not always know which was best for them. That confusion of character would work its way outward into their body and circumstances.

In this chapter we are concerned about the effects of separation from God on the body.

Mankind in this current day and culture identifies with his body in a great way. Food, medications, exercise programs, recreational sports, diets, items of comfort...we are obsessed with our bodies in western civilization.

And it is true that we have managed to increase our life expectancy in the past century far beyond the expectations of the previous millennium. But we have not begun to return to the life expectancies of the first men recorded in Genesis 5. Adam lived 930 years. His son Seth lived 912 years and his grandson Enos lived 905 years. Life was progressively driven out by the forces of death at work in beings who had separated themselves from oneness with Life Himself. Devolution took place from the perfection of creation.

This was not God's will. **God didn't put sickness and death upon humans because they disobeyed; He warned them against disobedience so that they would not bring upon themselves these effects of separation** spoken out against the devil and all who followed him into rebellion.

God and His Word are one. "In the beginning was the Word, and the word was with God and the Word was God"..."And the Word was made flesh" (John 1:1,14).

HE IS THE EVERLIVING POWER OF HIS OWN COMMUNICATION!

Can you see it? Can you see that when God has spoken out something, what has been spoken brings Itself to pass because He and His Word are one?

When we are told that God smote someone or made someone sick, the Word of the consequence of sin was what happened to them.

God is not sitting in a throne somewhere with a blessings spray and a curses spray arbitrarily spraying out blessings and curses, or even personally facilitating them. He has spoken out curses on that which is separate from Himself – from that which is other than Goodness and Love and Wisdom and Peace and Joy – and He has spoken out blessings on those who make a choice to align themselves with Him. So the Word spoken and coming to pass IS God doing it but in the sense that "For ever, O Lord, thy word is settled in heaven" (Psalm 119:89). This is the same Word of which it is said, "He sent His Word and healed them, and delivered them from their destructions" (Psalm 107 :20). It is why Jesus said for us to pray, "Thy Kingdom come, Thy will be done on earth as it is in heaven" (Matthew 6:10).

In Old Testament days, or under the Old Covenant that God made with Abraham, the way to receive physical healing was to do specific things in the sacrificial/priestly system. In New Testament days, or under the New Covenant made between the Father and Son, the way to receive physical healing is to have faith in The Sacrifice of the one who has become our High Priest forever.

Then why do we see Christians being sick?

Because we don't know God's will.

Because the father of lies has polluted the church's understanding so that we call evil good and good evil and don't know the difference. "My people are destroyed for lack of knowledge" (Hosea 4:6).

What is our answer?

Learning and having faith in God's promises.

135

The Apostle Peter teaches, "Whereby are given to us exceeding great and precious promises, that by these you might be partakers of the divine nature…" (II Peter 2:4).

God promises, "If Christ be in you, the body is dead because of sin but the Spirit is life because of righteousness; but if the Spirit of him that raised up Jesus from the dead dwell in you, **he that raised up Christ from the dead shall also quicken your mortal bodies by His Spirit that lives in you**" (Romans 8:10,11).

God promises, "…they shall lay hands on the sick, and they shall recover" (Mark 16:18).

God promises, "And the prayer of faith shall save the sick, and the Lord shall raise him up…" (James 5:15).

Can you believe God's promises of health to you? Or have you been so thoroughly taught that God may want you sick that your heart is filled with both good and evil beliefs about the nature of God?

One time a man sat in my kitchen shouting blasphemies against God. He was so filled with hatred that I could see a spirit of blasphemy in his eyes. His girlfriend who had brought him to our home for us to be a good influence on him was in horror and looked as though she expected lightning bolts to descend through the ceiling at any moment.

I shocked us all by what came out of my mouth.

"He's right," I said, wondering what was coming next and what I was doing, but following the leading of the Holy Spirit. The girlfriend looked as though she was now sure that his demons had gotten into me and we would both be fried momentarily.

"He's right to hate that thing that he thinks is God," I continued. "He has been told that it is God who puts cancer on people's mothers and kills little children in car wrecks. He has been taught that it is God who is causing sickness and misery of every kind in the earth. He has been taught the devil with a Jesus false face on."

I repeated, "He is right to hate that thing."

I was staring at the man while I spoke to his girlfriend and I saw the blasphemy leave as his eyes filled with tears. We all were silent for a moment and then very calmly he looked at me and quietly asked, "Can I hold your Bible?" I gave it to him and he looked reverently at it clasped in his hands. "It's been a lot of years since I held a Bible," he said.

Unfortunately, his concepts of God are similar to a large segment of the Church, although most of us are not so rebellious against the concept. Perhaps we should be.

On September 11, 2002 I heard a widow on the radio talking from one of the memorial services remembering the terrorist attacks of the previous year on the World Trade Center and the Pentagon. She said "I am so sick of hearing people say 'God had other plans for your husband. He is with God now. You must keep your faith. You can't lose your faith.' I am sorry but I had other plans…we had other plans. It's not hard to lose your faith at times like this– it's very easy to lose your faith." My heart ached for her and I turned to my husband "I want to talk to her and tell her that the people are wrong. It wasn't God who did it." I can just see the devil preening himself as people call him God.

That was not a sickness she was talking about, but the people who attempted to comfort her with that philosophy have the same mentality that calls sickness an act of God.

God has set the church against sickness. But we won't join the army and fight it until we are settled in our own mind what His will is concerning sickness.

God said to the Israelites "I call heaven and earth to record this day against you, that I have set before you life and death, blessing and cursing: therefore choose life, that both your and your seed may live" (Deuteronomy 30:19).

That word is forever settled in heaven. God has given you a choice. But you can't make a choice unless you know there is a choice to make.

God says, "Woe unto them that call evil good, and good evil..." (Isaiah 5:20).

He was not saying, "If you call evil good, I am going to cause you to have bad things happen in your life." He was saying, "If you call evil good, you will be causing evil things to come into your life." In other words, if you don't know God's will for you and the devil's will for you, you may very well cooperate with the devil and bring his will to pass.

"My people are destroyed for a lack of knowledge" (Hosea 4:6). God forgive us for the heresy about God's nature that we have allowed to permeate the Church of the Lord Jesus Christ and become tradition which makes His Word of no effect (Matt.15:6).

Recently there was a very serious flu in our area. Twice, ten days apart, I felt symptoms begin to creep into my head and throat and over my body. Within a few seconds both times, I spoke aloud.

"Jesus bore my sicknesses and carried my diseases and by His stripes I am healed. I will not receive these symptoms of flu!" And the symptoms left IMMEDIATELY! I was telling a friend of mine about this and he shared that he had the same experience once during the same time period.

Why did this happen for us when other Christians had been sick for weeks? I can guarantee you that neither of us is more generous or kind or good or loving or obedient than some of the Christians in bed with flu.

It happened because we believed it was not God's will for us to be sick! Really believed it. There was no trace of a niggling thought in the back of our minds of, "Maybe God wants me to have this flu so I can get some rest." We believed in His desire for our health without wavering even a tiny bit and we spoke out that belief.

The Lord said, "My people perish for a lack of knowledge" (Hosea 4:6). Please understand this verse. God's people are being destroyed because we have not been taught to know God's will.

The spiritual battle against sickness is like every other spiritual battle. What you believe in your heart and speak with your mouth will come to pass. Study God's Word in the area of healing until you know that you know that you know that God wants you healthy in the earth, as you will be in heaven.

In fact He not only wants but needs you healthy in the earth so He can demonstrate Himself in you and through you. He became sick once with the sickness due to all of us because of our fallen nature (Matthew 8:17) but He left that sickness when He was resurrected. There is no sickness in heaven. You are part of His physical body in the earth and He needs every member of that Body functioning well. You are redeemed from the curse of the law, which includes "every sickness and every plague" (Deut. 28:61).

God's will for you is a healthy body. May His will be done on earth as it is in heaven.

THINGS TO REMEMBER

The Battle Against Sickness

1. God is Jehovah Rapha, the God that heals you.

2. Jesus Christ bore your sickness and carried your diseases on the cross.

3. You are redeemed from the curse of the law, which includes every sickness and disease.

4. God is the ever living power of His own communication.

5. Put His Word in your mouth.

Scripture Truths

"Bless the Lord, O my soul, and forget not all his benefits…who heals all your diseases."
Psalm 103:2,3

" I have set before you life and death, blessing and cursing: therefore choose life, that both you and your seed may live."
Deuteronomy 30:19

"… if the Spirit of him that raised up Jesus from the dead dwell in you, <u>he that raised up Christ from the dead shall also quicken your mortal bodies by His Spirit that lives in you</u>."
Romans 8:10,11

"…the prayer of faith shall save the sick, and the Lord shall raise him up."
James 5:15

"He sent His Word and healed them…"   Psalm 107:20

"Jesus Christ is the same yesterday, and today, and forever."
Hebrews 13:8

BY HIS STRIPES YOU WERE HEALED.
Isaiah 53:5; I Peter 2:24

Chapter Thirteen

The Battle Against Broken Relationships

"Behold, how good and how pleasant it is for brethren to dwell together in unity."

Psalm 133:1

Before we get into specific relational problems, I want to address the nature and cause of all broken relationships.

If you read the story of the man and woman in the Garden of Eden told in Genesis 2 and 3, you will see that the man had a relational choice.

I refer to the couple in the garden as the man and woman instead of calling them Adam and Eve because they were both called Adam before the fall (Gen. 3:20). It was Adam who called his wife's name Eve after the fall. (Genesis 5:2; Genesis 3:20) They were one unit, in perfect relationship with each other and with God.

God had told the man, before the creation of the woman, not to eat the fruit of the tree of the knowledge of good and evil (Genesis 2:17). We find out in I Timothy 2:14 that the man was not deceived about the nature of their action. The woman was deceived and believed the enemy's communication that God had lied to them because He wanted to withhold some good thing from them (Genesis 3:4,5).

We have somehow gotten the idea that the man was off somewhere while this temptation, deception, and rebellion took place, but the Bible tells us, "she took of the fruit and ate and gave also to her husband there with her; and he did eat" (Genesis 3:6).

The man was not deceived and he was not unaware of what was going on. He was right there and knew that the consequences of partaking of that fruit would separate them from God and there would be bad consequences. But he chose to do so anyway. Why? The woman chose to partake and separate herself from oneness with God through her ignorance of truth. When she did so she separated herself from her husband who was still one with God and thus brought about a broken relationship with her husband.

Then the man had a choice. He could have stayed in relationship with God and lost the oneness with her. He chose a broken relationship with God over a broken relationship with his wife. But of course without God, every relationship has lost the ingredient that insures wholeness and the man did not maintain a perfect relationship with her either.

That choice is made over and over again - people choosing people over God.

Wrong choices between God's ways or selfish ways are the basis for broken relationships of every kind: marital, friendships, parent-child, business associates.

And very often people get angry when other people make the right choice and choose God over themselves, God's ways over the established world ways.

Because our world is fallen away from oneness with God, every relationship has within itself the seeds of destruction. Unless God is given Lordship over any relationship, there will be problems. And even when God is made Lord over a relationship, the devil will continue to try to divide and conquer and rid the relationship of that protection.

Initiating, maintaining, or reinstating the Lordship of Jesus over relationships is the key to victory over broken relationships.

We know that Jesus is called the Prince of Peace (Isaiah 9:6) so why would He make the statement "Think not that I am come to send peace on earth: I came not to send peace, but a sword. For I am come to set a man at variance against his father, and the daughter against her mother, and the daughter in law against her mother in law. And a man's foes shall be they of his own household" (Matthew 10:34-36).

???

Jesus, the Prince of Peace –Prince of harmony and oneness – says He came not to send peace but a sword.

Why would Jesus say such a thing?

Because of the original choice made in the garden: humans have put humans – self and others - before God ever since that time.

God wants no rivals; He wants each person to choose Him over a spouse, child, parent, or any other human.

What is the sword that Jesus sends instead of peace?

"...the sword of the Spirit, which is the Word of God..." (Ephesians 6:17).

"and out of His mouth goes a sharp sword..." (Revelation 19:14).

"The Word of God is alive and powerful and sharper than any two edged sword, piercing even to the dividing asunder of soul and spirit, and of the joints and marrow, and is a discerner of the thoughts and intents of the heart" (Hebrews 4:12).

Jesus came to bring a sword of division. The Word of God will divide us from things and people who are not one with Himself....if we will let Him.

But this chapter is about battle against broken relationships. How can we fight against a broken relationship if God Himself has done it?

The same God who said, "a man's foes will be of his own household" also promised "Believe on the Lord Jesus Christ, and you shall be saved, and your house" (Acts 16:31).

God wants to separate you from them if they are not walking with Him in His Word. He wants to make you one with Himself so that then you can become part of His salvation process. He wants to separate them from the world so they can become one with Himself. If you are more connected to Him, you can be a part of His salvation.

For this purpose, God has made many promises.

MARRIAGE

There are promises about marriage. In I Peter 3:1-7, some of the mysteries of the marriage relationship are revealed. We are told that if wives voluntarily cooperate with their husbands, the husbands will see their good behavior and be won to the Word of God. Sara is given as an example of this cooperation, so we should keep in mind that Sara had her own ideas about things, and once when Abraham differed with her, God said, "in all that Sarah has said to you, listen to her" (Genesis 21:12).

This admonition to "obey" a husband obviously does not include going against the will of God. Peter said to Sapphira, "How could you have agreed with your husband to tempt the Spirit of the Lord?"(Acts 5:9). And David said to Abigail when she went against her husband's wishes and behind his back to take provisions to David and his men "Blessed be the Lord God of Israel which sent you this day to meet me" (I Samuel 25:32).

A wife is to put obedience to God and His Word first and then, as part of the Body of Christ, as part of the ministry of the Lord Jesus, submit herself to loving her

145

husband and thus win him to obedience to the Word by her behavior.

In that passage in I Peter 3, husbands are told to dwell with their wives, giving them honor and recognizing that they are heirs together of the grace of life. It says that this honor and recognition are necessary to keep their prayers from being hindered. God calls husbands to choose Him first and then honor their wives, but they are not to give in to their wives' wrong choices like the very first husband in the Garden of Eden did.

When we put God first and enter into the ministry of Jesus to others, the relational brokenness becomes His concern. If we are one with Him, then when the other person becomes one with Him, relationship is restored or completed or, most likely, made to be what it was supposed to be in the first place.

What about divorce?

There is hardly a person in America who has not been affected in a personal way by divorce. And some of the effects of divorce are confusing.

I have seen some people who have waged a successful battle against divorce and, by what seems like a miracle of God, restored their broken relationship. I have seen others still waging a war to recover a marriage when the former spouse has gone on to a happy second marriage. I have seen people leave a marriage and receive great blessings from God. I have seen people stay in a marriage and be miserable. I have seen people leave a marriage and be miserable.

We are told that God hates divorce. But do we really know what constitutes divorce? Do we know what constitutes marriage?

The apostle Paul wrote some very interesting comments in I Corinthians, Chapter 6 while he was talking about marriage.

In verse 8 "Therefore I say to the <u>unmarried and widows</u> it is good for them if they stay even as I but if they cannot contain, let them marry…"

In verse 10 "And to <u>the married</u> I command, yet <u>not I but the Lord</u> let not the wife depart from her husband but if she depart let her remain unmarried or be reconciled to her husband, and let not the husband put away his wife."

In verses 12 - 16 "But <u>to the rest</u> , <u>speak I not the Lord</u> , if a brother has a wife that does not believe…..and the woman which has a husband that does not believe…..let them not depart for how do you know whether you may save…husband…wife."

This passage definitely points out three categories of marital status.

1.   Those who are single, who have never been married or have been married and widowed.

2.   The married people, whom God says must not dissolve their union even if they live apart.

3.   The rest, who consist of one believer and one unbeliever who have obviously gone through a legal ceremony and are called husband and wife. They are not considered married by God. This is simply a legalized partnership and has nothing to do with marriage as God sees it. God does not address what these people should do if they are unhappy but Paul, making sure that it is known that the advice does not come from God, thinks the Christian should stay and be a vessel of God's love to bring the other to salvation.

This is not the only time that God's Word goes against our traditional thinking.

In II Corinthians Chapter 6 Paul writes "Be not unequally yoked together with unbelievers for what fellowship does righteousness have with unrighteousness? What communion does light have with darkness? And what concord has Christ with Belial or what part has the believer with an infidel? And what agreement has the temple of God with idols (Verses 14 – 16)?

This scripture is used over and over again in counseling Christians against marrying non-Christians. I think it also includes business partnerships and other connections we make in life, but the passage most definitely has been agreed by the church to apply to marriage. Why then do we not accept the admonition of God that follows? "Wherefore come out from among them, and be separate, says the Lord, and touch not the unclean, and I will receive you" (verse 17).

Come out from among them. That is pretty strong language. Not exactly the way Paul presented it when he said he, not God, was speaking about the union between believers and unbelievers, advising the believer to stay.

And what constitutes a "believer"? The word believe in the Greek language, used here and in John 3:16 "whosoever believes in Him shall not perish but have everlasting life" does not mean "give mental assent to the fact" of Jesus' life. It means "trust in and rely on" Him. Sometimes we have church members who are not believers.

I pointed out these things because when it comes to having faith to keep a marriage together, a spiritual warrior must know whether it is a marriage in the eyes of God or simply a legal contract.

Our society today is inundated with romantic ideas of marriage that have nothing to do with scriptural representation of that state. The Bible speaks more of commitment than of feeling in the area of marital relations.

In Genesis 29 through 35, we see the story of Jacob and his marriages. Jacob fell in love with Rachel. He was deceived into marrying her older sister Leah first and then won Rachel as well. Neither the love or the deception negated the legitimacy of the marriage to Leah. In our society we would say that the state of Jacob's heart would show the true wife. And yet when we look at the story we see that it was Leah who bore Judah, the line that produced David and Jesus. And it was Leah with whom Jacob chose to be buried (Gen. 49:29 – 31).

Rachel, the beloved one, was the thief and idolator who took her father's household gods when the family left his home. She brought idolatry into Jacob's household. And it looks like she may have been an idol of sorts to Jacob.

In Genesis 32:28, God said "Thy name shall be called no more Jacob but Israel..." And yet all through the rest of that chapter and through chapters 33 and 34, he is called Jacob. In chapter 35, Rachel died and was buried. Watch now what happened... "And **Jacob** set a pillar upon her grave: that is the pillar of 'Rachel's grave unto this day. And **Israel** journeyed, and spread his tent beyond the tower of Edar" (Genesis 35:20,21). When Rachel was no longer in Jacob's life, he was able for the first time to walk in his new name.

In Ephesians 5, Paul says that Christian wives and husbands are to reflect the relationship between Christ and the Church. This is a calling and has nothing to do with feelings. It has to do with commitment to God and commitment to acts of love and goodness. And in order to walk in our new name of Christian – those who are like Christ – we must rid our lives of those things that hinder us.

If a person knows that their marriage is a true marriage in the eyes of God, and if they know that God is first in their own heart and their desire for the marriage relationship is not idolatry (we will discuss idolatry further in a later chapter) then they have all the forces of heaven with them. They can pray, knowing what God's will is, and knowing that the partner who does not cooperate for harmony in the marriage is deceived. They can then command the enemy away from the one with whom they are one flesh (Ephesians 5:31). They can love the erring spouse and be obedient to the admonitions of God concerning their own behavior, knowing that the Lord will bring about the harmony desired.

The Protestant Church does not differentiate between types of marriages and often penalizes a Christian who made a wrong choice, has repented, and is fully restored to relationship with God. The Roman Catholic Church has a process which investigates and, if it so finds, pronounces an annulment …a statement that there never was a marriage in the eyes of God. The persons granted an annulment are then free to get on with life without further penalty. Where there has been no marriage in God's eyes, there is no divorce in the eyes of God.

It would behoove us to follow Jesus' advice and "Judge not, that you be not judged" (Matthew 7:1). We don't know everything about the hearts and actions of everyone. And as Paul said, "Judge nothing before the time, until the Lord comes, who both will bring to light the hidden things of darkness, and will make manifest the counsels of the hearts..." (I Cor. 4:5).

What about adultery? Adultery is when one partner denies the oneness of the marital relationship to become one on some level with another person. This includes physical and/or emotional oneness with someone other than the spouse.

Is it possible to restore a marriage to what it should be when adultery has taken place?

Yes! Nothing is impossible for God. And I have seen marriages restored and even made better after a couple works through adultery to the other side.

It is very difficult when the wronged spouse views the adultery as a sin only against themselves, and not a sin against God. Hurt feelings and the pain of betrayal can bring in self-pity and bitterness, which are also sins that effectively block God out. And when that happens no one in the marriage is trusting Him for solutions. The wronged spouse must maintain an attitude of God's unconditional love and desire to see the offending spouse set free from the sin that has trapped his or her mind, emotions, and/or body. This is very difficult and one of the times when it is essential to "cast down imaginations and every high thing that exalts itself against the knowledge of God, bringing every thought into captivity to the obedience of Christ" (II Cor. 10:5).

What does it mean to bring every thought into captivity to the obedience of Christ? It means to forgive. "God was in Christ, reconciling the world unto himself, not imputing their trespasses unto them; and has committed unto us the word of reconciliation" (II Cor. 5:19). God has committed to us, to all Christians, the word of forgiveness and He wants to be in you not imputing the sin to the one who sins against you. It is God's unconditional love, not holding sins against anyone, that sets people free and heals relationships.

CHILDREN

And what about children? In our modern culture there are so many opportunities for strife between parents and children. Divorce often pits a child against one parent or another. Drugs, alcohol, and immoral lifestyles, like the Pied Piper, lead our young people out to drown in a sea of destruction.

There are promises in God's Word that have great spiritual power to regain children from the clutches of the enemy.

First of all, in Isaiah there is a promise made to the resurrected Jesus "And all your children shall be taught of the Lord, and great shall be the peace of your children" (Isaiah 54:13). If you are in Christ Jesus, that promise is to you. In Psalm 112 it says of the one who reveres the Lord, "His seed shall be mighty on the earth" (verse 2).

And you have the promise in Galatians 3:13 that you are redeemed from the curse of the law which includes:

"Your sons and your daughters shall be given to another people, and your eyes shall look and fail with longing for them all the day long; and there shall be no might in your hand" (Deut. 28:32). I have seen redemption from that curse work in many custody suits where God's will was that the children be raised in the home which was a more Christian environment than the normal placement that the courts would have made. I have never had to use it in a kidnapping but definitely it should be used to prevent kidnapping.

"You shall beget sons and daughters, but you shall not enjoy them, for they shall go into captivity." (Deut. 28:41). It's a curse for your children to be in any kind of captivity – to drugs, alcohol, and other immorality. You are redeemed from that curse, and the Sword of God's Word in the mouth of faith will sever them from those things.

I have seen this scripture come to pass in situations where it looked like estrangement would never end between parent and child. "Lift up your eyes round about and see: all they gather themselves together, they come to you. Your sons shall come from far and your daughters shall be nursed at your side" (Isaiah 60:4).

God wants family relationships to be harmonious. The last verse in the Old Testament promises that He will send the prophet Elijah, "before the coming of the great and dreadful day of the Lord, **and he shall turn the heart of the fathers to the children and the heart of the children to their fathers** lest I come and smite the earth with a curse" (Malachi 4:6).

God wants your family in harmony with one another. Trust that His will is the restoration of family love; trust

Him to bring it about as you walk in forgiveness and obedience and faith in His promises.

OTHERS

Strife can happen between any two people or groups of people. It can happen in marriages, in families, in friendships, between neighbors or co-workers, in the supermarket or driving down the highway.

The apostle Paul tells us what happens during strife: "the servant of God must not strive; but be gentle to all, apt to teach, patient, instructing in meekness those who are oppositional, in hope that God will give them repentance to know the truth and that they may arouse themselves out of the snare of the devil, who are taken captive by him at his will" (II Timothy 2:24 – 26). When we get into strife, we are taken captive by the devil.

I remember one time when I belonged to an independent church denomination – every individual church being on its own as to constitution and procedure. Some of the members of the Board voted to ask the pastor to leave – and did so - but the regulations made when the church was established did not allow that. The procedure to be followed was that a majority vote of the congregation was required for such an action. The congregation was very upset. The majority wanted the pastor to stay. There was a meeting at the church and the Board agreed to allow one person to be spokesperson to address the Board on behalf of the gathered congregation of hundreds of concerned people.

The Board ended up conceding that they were wrong and withdrew the request to the pastor. Of course the damage was done and the pastor resigned a few months later.

But the thing that happened to me during that time took place outside the church after the meeting. There were groups gathered all over the church lawn, arguing different points of the situation. I was among them.

Suddenly it was like in a movie when the crowd fades into the background and a moment of focus happens. I saw things from a God's Eye View. I saw His children bitter and pointing fingers and red faced and shouting. And I saw that if non-Christians drove by, that's what the Church would present to them. And I saw that God's heart was concerned much more with our strife than with our regulations.

That was over thirty years ago and there are people now who are still hurting and not in Church fellowship because of the way that situation was handled. When we are in strife, we are taken captive by the devil at his will.

The writer of Hebrews says, "Follow peace with all men, and holiness without which no man shall see the Lord, looking diligently lest any man fall from the grace of God, lest any root of bitterness springing up trouble you and thereby many be defiled" (Hebrews 12:14,15).

Many are defiled when we have bitterness in our hearts. We are to walk in the grace of God, being instruments of reconciliation, but we can't do that with bitterness toward others. And we can't get rid of emotional bitterness by ourselves. Many times, by an act of my will, I have asked God, the Gardener of my soul (John 15:2) to pull out a root of bitterness. When I have done that, I do my part by speaking and acting as if there was no bitterness. And soon I find that it is no longer there. The situation may be the same; I may not like what is going on; but the bitterness that poisons the situation and keeps God from moving in it is gone.

In my opinion, the greatest passage about relational behavior is in the 4th chapter of Ephesians.

"Let no corrupt communication proceed out of your mouth but that which is good to the use of edifying, that it may minister grace unto the hearers" (Eph. 4:29). Every word we speak should be for the purpose of ministering grace, undeserved favor, to others. Paul says that this will ensure that we don't do what the next verse says.

"And grieve not the Holy Spirit of God, whereby you are sealed unto the day of redemption" (verse 30). The Holy Spirit of God is called the Spirit of Grace (Heb.10:29); He is God's grace poured out in the earth. And we in the church are the vessels through whom He moves and speaks. It literally grieves Him when we speak accusations and hate because He IS grace and love.

Paul continues, "Let all bitterness, and wrath, and anger, and clamour, and evil speaking, be put away from you, with all malice; and be kind to one another, tenderhearted, forgiving one another, even as God for Christ's sake has forgiven you" (verses 31 and 32).

For Christ's sake God has forgiven you...we tend to think that means "for the sake of Jesus". But there is much more to it than that. Christ means the anointing. If you are a Christian, you are an anointed one. He forgave you in order that His own character and nature could be reproduced in you. We who are Christians are to allow His nature to flow through us and reproduce itself in others. When we are opposing the grace of God for any person or group of people, we are rebelling against the accomplished work of Jesus Christ on the cross and causing grief to the Holy Spirit who came to administer the results of that work. He forgives us for the sake of the anointing to restore Shalom.

We in this world are so concerned with who is right and what our rights are that we turn away from His righteousness, which is always grace and forgiveness.

Grace and forgiveness on the part of one person does not always restore a broken relationship. Only God can do that, and only with the cooperation of all the parties involved.

As I said before in the chapter on the Battle Against Unforgiveness, the person has to know that they need forgiveness. And they need to want the relationship before a right relationship can be restored.

In this world where each person has been given the gift of free will by their Creator, He won't - and we are not to - control the wills, emotions, and minds of others, no matter how much we may want that. To do so is witchcraft – controlling through mental power - though it goes by many names such as manipulation, brainwashing, and tyranny.

If another person does not want a harmonious relationship with you, God will not force them to it. And you should not either. There is a popular saying "If you love something set it free. If it comes back to you, it is yours forever. If it doesn't, it was never yours to begin with."

All Christian relationships are not perfect and it is not always going to be that all relationships will be restored. "And Barnabas determined to take John Mark with them, but Paul thought it not good....and the contention was so sharp between them that they departed asunder one from the other; and so Barnabas took Mark...and Paul chose Silas" (Acts 15:37– 40). Paul and Barnabas departed from each other and yet the Holy Spirit went with both parties and spread grace throughout their journeys.

God does not want contention and bitterness; God cannot move through contention and bitterness. Sometimes a restored relationship necessitates geographical distance between the two parties. Spiritual harmony does not require physical affection or affinity and it does not require agreement on all things.

Spiritual harmony does require walking in grace toward all men.

One time when I was praying I sensed the Spirit of the Lord telling me to get on my knees and say the Lord's prayer. I did and then felt "Again" so I said it aloud again. After about fifty times of saying The Lord's Prayer aloud, I got what He wanted me to see. There is not one time that "mine" or "me" is mentioned, only "our" and "us" (Matthew 6:9-13).

To pray the way Jesus teaches me, I cannot ask for my daily bread without asking for yours too. I cannot ask for forgiveness without acknowledging your right to be forgiven. I cannot ask to be delivered from evil without asking that you be delivered too.

I cannot acknowledge God as my Father without acknowledging Him as yours too.

God wants all His children to be in relational harmony. But that cannot happen until each of those children is in right relationship to Him.

We need to be praying for all mankind to be in right relationship with God. Right relationship with one another is dependent on that basic rightness with Him.

THINGS TO REMEMBER

The Battle Against Broken Relationships

1. God wants all mankind to live in peace with Him and each other.

2. If yours is a marriage in God's eyes, you have promises to insure it's security.

3. You are redeemed from being powerless with your children.

4. Walking in grace toward others is the greatest spiritual warfare.

5. Refusing to speak angry or bitter words is to cooperate with the Spirit of Grace.

6. Our Father...Deliver us from evil.

Scripture Truths

"When a man's ways please the Lord, He makes even his enemies to be at peace with him."   Proverbs 16:7

"Believe on the Lord Jesus Christ, and you shall be saved, and your house."   Acts 16:31

"Let no corrupt communication proceed out of your mouth but that which is good to the use of edifying, that it may minister grace unto the hearers. And grieve not the Holy Spirit of God, whereby you are sealed unto the day of redemption. Let all

158

bitterness, and wrath, and anger, and clamour, and evil speaking, be put away from you, with all malice; and be kind to one another, tenderhearted, forgiving one another, even as God for Christ's sake has forgiven you."   Eph. 4:29- 32

"Follow peace with all men, and holiness without which no man shall see the Lord, looking diligently lest any man fall from the grace of God, lest any root of bitterness springing up trouble you and thereby many be defiled."   Hebrews 12:14,15

"BELOVED, LET US LOVE ONE ANOTHER FOR LOVE IS OF GOD."   I John 4:7

Chapter Fourteen

The Battle Against Shame

"But thou, O Lord, art a shield for me; my glory, and the lifter up of mine head." Psalm 3:3

Saint Bernard of Clairvaux made an astonishing statement about love. He wrote that there are four degrees, or progressions, of love.

1. Man loves self for self's sake.
2. Man loves God for self's sake.
3. Man loves God for God's sake.
4. Man loves self for God's sake.

We have a difficult time with that last one. Most of us have been taught that it is selfish to love ourselves at all.

And yet it is God who tells us to love others as we love ourselves (Matthew 22:39). But if we do not learn to love ourselves in the right way, we will not learn to love others in the right way.

I believe that anyone who has ever done much Christian counseling, whether a pastor, a professional counselor, or just with friends, knows that the Body of Christ, the Church, is riddled with shame. And shame is the opposite of self love.

The words translated "shame" in both the Greek and Hebrew all give the connotation of feeling confusion and worthlessness. The New World Dictionary defines shame as "a painful feeling of having lost the respect of others because of the improper behavior, incompetence, etc. of oneself or another."

Shame is a feeling of worthlessness because somebody did something wrong.

Shame can be experienced because a person has been a victim. Many abuse victims feel shame because they think they must have done something to cause the abuse, or at the least neglected to do something to avoid the abuse. Sometimes the victim believes that they deserve the abuse because of their own actions or inaction. There is confusion along with the guilt because of the inability to place blame where it belongs.

Self hatred seems on the rise in today's world, even among Christians. Self hatred is the next step beyond shame.

We have already looked at the battle against confusion and have seen that it partly includes not knowing where we stand. This is the part of confusion that is involved in shame.

The other part of shame is feelings of worthlessness.

In Anger Resolution Workshops we look at a universal truth: BEHIND ALL DESTRUCTIVE ANGER IS SOME FEAR.

What does this have to do with shame?

Behind all fear is some degree of shame. How many times have you seen someone get angry with you because they are wrong? Anger at being wrong happens when people are insecure, when they have feelings of shame and worthlessness.

In order to understand shame, we also need to understand another truth:

DEPRESSION IS ANGER TURNED INWARD.

Fear is a result of shame. It can manifest itself outwardly as anger trying to blame others or it can turn inward and blame self. Fear is a result of feeling vulnerable and confused and lacking in self worth because of something that has happened.

Wrong Action>Feeling of inadequacy>Shame>Fear>Anger at results of Wrong

It began in the Garden when the first humans fell away from oneness with God. As soon as their souls were polluted with a mixed nature, being one with both good and evil, they saw themselves without the righteousness of God and were afraid.

"And they heard the voice of the Lord God....and Adam and his wife hid themselves from the presence of the Lord God...and the Lord God called to Adam and said to him 'Where are you?' and he said 'I heard your voice in the garden, and I was afraid, because I was naked, and I hid myself" (Genesis 3: 8-10).

"I was afraid because I was naked...and I hid myself." How many times has that scene been played out by all of us?

Fear comes from shame and shame comes from inadequacy.

The state of fallen mankind is one of inadequacy. We who were created in the image of God fell away from that image. We instinctively know what we are created to be: beings filled with love and joy and peace. And we instinctively know that we fall short of that. So what is the answer to our state? How can we be free from shame?

As the verse in Psalms said at the opening of this chapter, God is our shield, our glory, and the lifter up of our heads from shame.

Jesus bore your sin on the cross of Calvary. "The Lord laid on him the iniquity of us all" (Isaiah 53:6). We have never fully gotten the revelation of that...none of us. I know it with my head but I am still making room for it in my heart.

One of my favorite times of pastoral counseling was with a 12 year old boy. He was very intelligent but had Attention Deficit Disorder which resulted in some learning challenges. The bad self image led to other behavior problems and he was always behind in his school work and always in trouble. He was very depressed and called himself a "doody" boy, meaning "poo poo" or excrement. "I'm just a doody boy," he would say hopelessly.

We talked for a while and then I was led to share my own conversion experience with him. I read him II Corinthians 5:21 "For He has made him to be sin for us, who knew no sin; that we might be made the righteousness of God in him."

Then I said, "In regular people language that verse says that on the cross God made Jesus into a doody boy so that you can become the goodness and wisdom of Jesus."

I don't know that I have ever seen such joy immediately flood anyone's features and drive out despair so effectively.

I said, "Would you like to invite Jesus into your heart to start doing that in you?" Not only did he receive Jesus right then and there but he jumped up and ran out of the room to where his family was waiting, grabbed his sister and said, "Come and listen to this!"

All shame did not immediately leave that boy's heart, no more than it all left the rest of our hearts at our rebirth, but he continued increasing in self esteem.

The enemy does not want you to be free from shame. He hates the truth that Jesus identified with you in your sin and bore it for you and that you have no cause for shame. He works hard to keep you ashamed, which is, according to the New World Dictionary, "feeling shame because something bad, wrong, or foolish was done."

The devil wants us to feel ashamed for a reason most of us would never suspect.

When one of my granddaughters was around 2 ½ years of age, we went to the church and were walking up the steps to the Sunday School area. Maggie was not accustomed to steps so I wanted to hold her hand as we walked. But like most 2 year olds she wanted to do it herself. I let her but watched carefully in case she should need my help. Sure enough, down she went. As I reached down to help her, she grinned at me. "Oops, Grammy, I dropped myself!" And she let me pick her up and put her back on her feet again. The next time she made it to the top without falling.

When Maggie fell, she laughed. It never occurred to Maggie that I would fuss at her for her inadequacies as a climber. She felt no shame for having fallen. It would have been ridiculous for Maggie to be angry with herself for not being able to climb stairs at 2 the way I could climb steps at 50. It would have been a wrong kind of pride.

When we feel shame we rarely realize that it is the reverse side of the same coin as pride, and that is one reason why the devil wants us ashamed. Shame says, "I have acted inadequately but I should be adequate. Therefore I am ashamed."

Humility says "I have acted inadequately because I am inadequate. I can do no good thing on my own, not in my own strength and not in my own righteousness."

But Paul writes, "not that I am adequate by myself to think anything of myself, but my adequacy is of God" (II Cor. 3:6).

The devil was lifted up with pride at his own nature (Ezekiel 28:17). We too are tempted by the pride of life (I

John 2:16). The enemy wants us to think that we are such wonderful, wise, and strong creatures that we should never "drop ourselves." But that is an impossibility.

Shame keeps us from laughing at ourselves and letting our heavenly Father pick us up and put us back on our feet. Shame says, "I should have never fallen down. Other people may fall but I should not have."

One time a friend of mine was berating herself because she had been trying to tame her tongue and had gone for several days without passing on a single negative thing about anyone, but then in one brief hour she had let loose and said a lot of negative things. She was in a state of despair and shame, feeling that God must be very disgusted with her. I breathed a quick prayer and this came out of my mouth. "Do you remember when your children were little and learning to walk?"

"Yes," she said.

"When your husband came home each day did you report how many times they fell?"

"No," she laughed. "I told him how many steps they had taken."

I said "And your heavenly parent is just the same. He's not looking at the falls but at how wonderful it was that you took so many steps without falling. Now get up again and keep on walking until it comes naturally."

Jesus was born a baby, an infant. He did not come out of the womb walking, much less walking on water. What makes us so arrogant as to think that we should be immediately perfect?

The devil also wants you to feel shame because when you feel shame, your focus is on you. Peter said, "Humble yourselves therefore under the mighty hand of God, that he may exalt you in due time; casting all your care upon him, for he cares for you" (I Peter 5:6,7).

When you humble yourself by recognizing that you are needy, just like all other human beings, God can lift you up and make you stand. Christians often quote Philippians 4:13: "I can do all things through Christ which strengthens me." But how often do we admit, "Without Him I can do nothing good."

Shame says you should have been able to do the good thing or resist the bad thing. Humility says, "Of course I did something bad, wrong, or foolish! That is my natural state of being." But then humility also says "Forgive me for that action and wash me from the cause of it that is in my heart."

"If we confess our sins He is faithful and just to forgive us our sins and cleanse us from all unrighteousness" (I John 1:9).

God makes some promises to those who are in Christ Jesus: "Fear not, for you shall not be ashamed; neither be confused for you shall not be put to shame; for you shall forget the shame of your youth" (Isaiah 54:4). He goes on to say, "No weapon that is formed against you shall prosper and every tongue that shall rise against you in judgment you shall condemn. This is the heritage of the servants of the Lord, and their righteousness is of me, saith the Lord" (Isaiah 54:17).

Shame is part of the coin of pride that says our righteousness should be of ourselves. Oh the joy of not having to worry about our righteousness and our reputations! "Who shall lay anything to the charge of God's elect? It is God that justifies" (Romans 8:33).

I wrote a little phrase years ago before I really understood it in my heart, and now it is one of the truest things I know.

HUMILITY IS NOT A VIRTUE. IT IS SIMPLY THE REALIZATION OF ONE'S TRUE STATE OF BEING.

"All have sinned and fallen short of the glory of God" (Romans 3:23).

If you understand your true state of being then you will never feel shame but will be able to look up and smile at the One who loves you unconditionally and say, "Oops, I dropped myself!" and let Him put you on your feet again.

Don't let the devil keep you focused on you and your failures instead of on the source of all goodness and success. God needs you emptied of focus on your self's abilities or inabilities so that He can fill you with Himself and His ability. Then not only will you forget the shame of your youth (Isaiah 54:4) but "for your shame, you will have double" (Isaiah 61:7). In other words, when you hand the Lord your inadequacies, you will be given twice as much of His glory.

"For both He that sanctifies and they who are sanctified are all of one; for which cause He is not ashamed to call them brothers" (Hebrews 2:11). If Jesus is not ashamed of you, don't you dare be ashamed of yourself!

Just keep looking at Him and, "beholding His glory, be changed into that same image from glory to glory by the Spirit of the Lord" (II Cor. 3:18).

He loves you. Love yourself. And let Him BE your righteousness.

If you could do it right, you wouldn't need a Savior.

THINGS TO REMEMBER

The Battle Against Shame

1. All mankind is fallen and all need God's righteousness.

2. Shame is an attempt by the devil to get you to concentrate on yourself and your inadequacies.

3. Humility is not a virtue but a realization of your true state of being.

4. God promises that when you depend on Him, you will be free from shame and walk in His glory.

5. Laugh at yourself and let God pick you up.

Scripture Truths

"But thou, O Lord, art a shield for me; my glory, and the lifter up of mine head."   Psalm 3:3

"not that I am adequate by myself to think anything of myself, but my adequacy is of God."   II Cor. 3:6

"Fear not, for you shall not be ashamed; neither be confused for you shall not be put to shame; for you shall forget the shame of your youth."   Isaiah 54:4

"Who shall lay anything to the charge of God's elect? It is God that justifies."   Romans 8:33

BUT WITH ME IT IS A VERY SMALL THING THAT I SHOULD BE JUDGED BY YOU, OR BY MAN'S JUDGMENT; YES, I DON'T EVEN JUDGE MYSELF.

I Cor. 4:3

Chapter Fifteen

The Battle Against Idolatry

"Little children, keep yourselves from idols."   I John 5:21

In looking at idolatry, we are going to be exposing the root cause of all of our problems in life.

What a bold statement! But it is true. Idolatry is having something that is more important to humans than God is.

The Greek word translated "idol" is literally something seen and worshipped.

How often have we heard or used the expression "My eyes were bigger than my stomach"? This problem has been going on since the beginning – mankind seeing and wanting things that they were incapable of handling.

In the garden, the woman looked at the tree which fruit God had forbidden them and she "<u>saw</u> that the tree was good for food, that it was <u>pleasant to the eyes</u>, and a tree to be desired to make one wise" (Genesis 3:6). She saw with her eyes and desired with her heart. She wanted what she saw more than she wanted to be obedient. But she was not equipped to handle that which she saw and desired.

It was not for His own sake that God wrote the first two commandments of the classic ten.

"Thou shalt have no other gods before me.

Thou shalt not make unto you any graven image or any likeness of any thing that is in heaven above, or that is in the earth beneath, or that is in the water under the earth; Thou shalt not bow down thyself to them nor serve them; for I the Lord thy God am a jealous God, visiting the iniquity of the fathers upon the children unto the third and fourth generation of them that hate me" (Ex. 20:3-5).

Here again we have some of that language that causes us to get a wrong picture of God. If God had just commanded us to put Him first, we would have no problem understanding that, but He said, "I the Lord thy God am a jealous God, visiting the iniquity of the fathers upon the children..." And we get a picture of the one on the throne, spraying down the sin of the fathers on the innocent children.

But just as we did in the battle against sickness, again we need to remember that God and His Word are one (John 1:1,14). What God has spoken out is still active and at work to bring itself to pass, to enflesh itself.

And God ordained from the beginning of Creation that everything would bring forth after its kind (Genesis 1:11,21,24). That Word of generation is still at work and the father's sin is still reproduced in the child's nature. Instead of being a threat that God would put a sin or its punishment on the child of a transgressor, God was warning that we should not put anything before Him because that idolatry would be passed on through the blood line to our descendants.

Idolatry is worship; it means to do homage to that which has attracted our eyes. An idol can be some thing or person, or it can be a representation of a thing, person, or system. We've all heard the expression about somebody "worshipping the almighty dollar." This does not mean that the person has set up a physical shrine or gets on their knees to a dollar sign or a dollar bill. It means that the person's lifestyle is designed with one goal in mind – the acquisition of money. When a person is worshipping God, their lifestyle is designed with the goal of acquiring more of God in their lives.

IDOLATRY CAN BE TOWARD A PERSON WHOSE PRESENCE IS MORE GREATLY DESIRED THAN GOD'S PRESENCE.

There have been several times in my own life where idolatry of persons has crept in. And this idolatry took different forms.

Once I think I would have stolen to provide something that one of my daughters wanted, a dress to wear to prom. That was putting her desire above God's law. As it turned out He provided what she wanted…but the lack went on long enough for me to recognize the idolatry – the sin in my heart.

Another time I recognized that I did what my husband wanted instead of what God wanted. The way some Christians interpret the Bible, they would say that God would want me to submit to my husband's wishes even if I thought differently about God's will in a matter. But I knew better… and still made that choice to disobey God because I wanted more to please my husband than God. That's idolatry and it is sin.

Another time I was separated from someone I loved deeply and found myself wanting to go to heaven more to see that person than to see Jesus. That is idolatry and it is sin.

Idolatry is worship of something we can see. And that seeing does not have to be with our physical eyes; it can be only in our minds. It doesn't have to be physical at all. Mental fantasizing about something that is forbidden to you is idolatry and it is sin.

Whenever <u>anything</u>, even something given to us by God, becomes more important to us than God, it is idolatry and it is sin.

There was a time when the Lord had me out of ministry. Nobody needed me and I felt useless. I prayed about it and heard nothing. I decided that I would just spend my time in intercession for people. I believed that by praying I would still be useful. Then God told me to stop my intercession for others.

I cannot even begin to tell you the agitation and dissatisfaction in my life at that period. I was not being useful to anyone in any way. I went to the Lord and asked Him why this was happening. And He asked me a question.

"What if I don't want you to do anything useful again ever? What if I just want you to sit at the piano and play love songs to Me?"

Gulp.

Not be useful ever again?

Then I saw it. I saw that I had made an idol of the picture of myself as a Servant. I remembered that even when I accepted Jesus, it was a package deal. I had said, "I give you my life and I ask you to use me to get miracles to people."

I had to recognize that I wanted the mental picture of me as a lover of God and servant to mankind more than I actually wanted God Himself. Even my worship of the true God was self-oriented. That was idolatry and it was sin.

Before we go farther, I want to specify the difference between a mental picture that is idolatry and one given from God. Proverbs 29:18 says, "Where there is no vision, the people perish." If we don't have a picture in our minds of what God wants, we are left vulnerable to every wrong picture the enemy would plant there.

If the couple in the garden had protected the picture God gave them of "in the day you eat it, you shall surely die", and believed that picture above the lies of the enemy or the desire for human companionship, the history of mankind in the earth would have been much different.

God gives His vision through words. Words paint a picture. A word is a thought communicated by one person to the mind of another person. God's word communicates His thoughts to your mind and paints a picture of how that particular word affects you.

God said, "I know the thoughts that I think toward you...thoughts of peace and not of evil, to give you hope and a future" (Jeremiah 29:13). If you read that and believe it, you will expect good things to happen in your future and will not be drawn off by pictures the devil plants. And the devil can definitely plant a picture that you think is God's will, but that will be opposite from that Word of God's in Jeremiah. I can think of several versions people buy of "I have called you to become a martyr for my sake." And they either believe they won't have a future or they see their future filled with chaos and evil. And, yes, the picture of ourselves as martyrs can be Idolatry in a big way, seeing ourselves as suffering unjustly and deserving much pity from others.

The devil also can make you think that something outside of God's will for you will make you happy, when the truth is that it will steal, kill, and destroy the wonderful future God has planned.

I have heard it said that whatever we think about when we are alone is what we truly worship.

What do you think about in your spare time? Your reputation? Your belongings? Your money? Your loved ones? Your career? Your leisure activities? Your good deeds? The wrongs done against you by others?

"The wrongs done against you by others?" Surely that didn't belong in a list of potential idolatries! Yes, it did.

We often play over and over in our minds the pictures of wrongs and hurts. We think about it, pour our emotional and mental energy into mulling over those circumstances and our own pain. We either drown in self-pity or swim vigorously through torrents of anger. That too is idolatry – putting what someone else does or has done before the promises of God for peace.

To worship, in its most basic meaning, is to bow down to something. When you mentally or emotionally or physically bow down to something, you are worshipping it.

I have seen people worship fear. They bow down to it and give in to its' demands instead of trusting the Lord.

I have seen people worship romance or sex. They bow down to it and give in to its' demands instead of obeying the Lord.

I have seen people worship leisure activities - sports, television, card games. They bow down to them and give into those demands on their time instead of serving the Lord.

I have seen people worship revenge. They bow down to it and fill their minds with it instead of submitting to the Lord's grace.

I have seen people worship people. They bow down to their wills instead of the will of the Lord.

I have seen people worship Self. They bow down to it and indulge it instead of allowing the Lord to mold it.

What do you worship?

You have a choice.

When we REALLY choose to obey the 1st commandment to have no other gods before the One True God, the other 9 commandments are more readily followed.

When God gives you a vision to bring to pass as part of His ministry in the earth, that picture is meant to be thought about. How then can we differentiate between meditating on a vision from God and idolatry?

If the very thing that He calls us to do or the very things He gives us to enjoy can become idols, how can we possibly ever get away from idolatry?

The answer to this is balance. We are to pursue the visions He gives us. We are to ask for and enjoy the things He gives us. But those visions and those things should never be more important to us that He Himself.

The devil is not a gentleman. He will try to keep you from receiving a vision or gift from God. Then if he can't do that, he will try to get you to make an idol of the vision or the dream. And if he can't do that he will try to make you feel guilty for enjoying the vision or gift.

At any time, you should be willing to give the vision God gave you to another for them to bring to pass in the earth - if He directs you to do so. At any time you should be willing to give the gift He gave you to someone else - if He so leads. By that willingness, you ensure that your relationship with God Himself is more important than any task He gives you or any gift He bestows.

He is to be your all in all. You are to be His beloved child ever receiving and ever obedient.

Keep your heart in balance. He wants you to enjoy life, but He wants you to know that He IS Life and that all good things are from Him. In your pursuit of your vision, recognize that all accomplishment is His. In your enjoyment of your gifts, remember their source.

THINGS TO REMEMBER

The Battle Against Idolatry

1. What you desire most is what you worship.

2. You can choose what to bow down to in your mind, emotions, and body.

3. God has a wonderful future planned for you; the enemy wants to mess it up.

4. The devil lies to you about what will make you happy.

5. What you think about when you are alone shows your priorities.

Scripture Truths

"Little children, keep yourselves from idols."
I John 5:21

"Thou shalt have no other gods before me. Thou shalt not make unto you any graven image or an likeness of any thing that is in heaven above, or that is in the earth beneath, or that is in the water under the earth; Thou shalt not bow down thyself to them nor serve them; for I the Lord thy God am a jealous God, visiting the iniquity of the fathers upon the children unto the third and fourth generation of them that hate me."
Ex. 20:3-5

"Where there is no vision, the people perish."
Proverbs 29:18

"Thou wilt keep him in perfect peace whose mind is stayed on thee: because he trusteth in thee." Isaiah 26:3

177

YOU SHALL LOVE THE LORD YOUR GOD WITH ALL YOUR HEART AND SOUL AND MIND AND STRENGTH.

Mark 12:30

Chapter Sixteen

The Battle Against Impurity

"The Lord shall establish thee an holy people unto Himself..."
Deut. 28:9

As we can see from this scripture, one of the blessings God promises His people is that we will be established in holiness. The word in Hebrew is Qadosh and means devoted or dedicated to the purpose of God.

Holiness is purity, without pollution of any kind.

God Himself is called Holy because He is completely devoted to His purposes without pollution of any kind, or as James put it, "with whom is no variableness, neither shadow of turning" (James 1:17).

Only complete holiness, complete dedication to your salvation, would have resulted in Jesus on the cross.

"Ruach Ha Qadosh" is "The Holy Spirit". God's Spirit poured out in the earth today "on all flesh" (Joel 2:28, Acts 2:17) is here for one purpose - to minister God's grace to every human being until they are changed into the likeness of God, just like mankind was created to be in the first place. His motivation is pure; He is completely

179

dedicated to that one purpose of establishing God's love, and that is why He is grieved when we speak and act outside of love with each other (Ephesians 4:29 – 32).

We, who often have many purposes, find that hard to understand. We have career goals and relationship goals and self-improvement goals and home and garden goals. We can't imagine being completely single-minded in purpose. And yet it is when a person is completely single-minded that they accomplish the things that other people seem to miss.

Those we have designated Saints, who brought themselves and their accomplishments to the attention of the world, were single minded in purpose. The Olympic gold medal winners and other world-renowned athletes have been single minded. Inventors and artists and writers, statesmen and clerics and scientists throughout the ages have made an impact on our society because they were single-minded in their purpose.

"For thus saith the high and lofty One that inhabits eternity, whose name is Holy; I dwell in the high and holy place, with him also that is of a contrite and humble spirit, to revive the spirit of the humble, and to revive the heart of the contrite ones" (Isaiah 57:15).

God says that His name is "Holy." A name means the character and nature of something and God tells us that His very character and nature is one that is devoted to a purpose. That purpose is to reproduce Himself in the physical world in His entirety. And He has chosen to reproduce Himself in and through human beings. "Of His own will He begat us with the Word of Truth, that we should be a kind of firstfruits of His creatures" (James 1:18).

God's intention in the beginning was that the race of mankind would be one with Him and perfectly reflect Him in the physical realm. That intention has not changed.

The only thing that changed was that since mankind went against the purpose of God and began to reflect the behavior and desires of His enemy, God's actions have had to accommodate that rebellion and accomplish His purpose with great cost to Himself.

That is why He said in the passage from Isaiah 57 that He lives "also with him who is of a contrite and humble spirit, to revive the spirit of the humble and revive the heart of the contrite one."

OUR PURPOSE IS TO BECOME ONE WITH GOD'S PURPOSES, TO BECOME ONE WITH HIM AND PERFECTLY REFLECT HIM IN THE PHYSICAL REALM.

The paradox is that this is to be our purpose but we cannot do a thing to bring it about.

This is why God says that He is with those who are humble and contrite. We discussed humility before and saw that true humility is to recognize our need for God and ask Him for it. "Blessed are the poor in spirit; for theirs is the kingdom of heaven" (Matthew 5:3). This was the first of the group of sayings by Jesus that we call the Beatitudes, the first sentence of His discourse that we have named the Sermon on the Mount. We have to recognize our need for God's Spirit, for His nature and character, before we can enter into the kingdom of heaven.

"He has delivered us from the power of darkness and translated us into the kingdom of his dear Son" (Colossians 1:13). The power of darkness is the deception that we do not need God, that we are such wonderful creatures, as we are, that we do not need to change. The kingdom of His dear Son is the kingdom of light that sees and receives all from God.

The second Beatitude is, "Blessed are they that mourn; for they shall be comforted" (Matthew 5:4). This has to do with contrition. The New World Dictionary defines contrite as "feeling deep sorrow or remorse for having sinned or done wrong."

In our society today we have become experts for excusing, justifying, and explaining away sins and wrongdoing. Having a contrite heart has gone out of style. But that is where God is, "with him who is of a contrite and humble spirit...to revive the heart of the contrite one."

When we become single minded concerning our oneness with God, we will mourn the sinfulness in our lives, we will experience deep remorse for having sinned or done wrong.

I committed a sin over three decades ago that I had asked God for forgiveness about. He forgave me and yet one day recently I knew there was something wrong inside and it concerned that part of my life.

I asked my prayer/accountability partner to pray with me. I knew God had forgiven me, so what was the problem...what was the burden I was experiencing? I held up that sin to Him and began to see the things that had happened to others and to myself because of it. I began to weep, and I continued weeping until my friend feared I would hyperventilate. But finally it was over and I was calm and the heavy place I felt in my heart was gone. True contrition had taken place and therefore I could receive the forgiveness that God had already and readily given me. His Love filled that part of my heart that had that sin hidden away from my own understanding. I had mentally received forgiveness but shame and fear had kept me from receiving it in my heart.

The paradox of our inability to accomplish oneness with God is overcome by God Himself in the presence of the Holy Spirit poured out in the earth.

It is He who brings us to a recognition of sin and righteousness and judgment....and of the need for contrition! And He is such a gentleman that He does it only when we can emotionally handle it.

Jesus said that He would send the Comforter "And when he is come, he will reprove the world of sin, and of righteousness, and of judgment" (John 16:8).

I want us to look very carefully at what the Holy Spirit is here to reprove, or convince/convict, the world about.

"Of sin because they do not believe on me" (John 16:9). Whether we want to believe this or not, the only sin the Holy Spirit is convicting people of is the sin of not trusting in and relying on Jesus. That lack of trust and reliance may be by those who have never acknowledged their need of a Savior. The lack of trust and reliance may be by those who have accepted His sacrifice to receive rebirth but are not looking to Him to meet their ongoing spiritual, mental, emotional, physical, financial, or social needs. The only reason the Holy Spirit is going to convict someone of a wrong is because it is an idol substituted for Jesus Christ in their lives.

"...Of righteousness because I go to my Father, and you see me no more" (John 16:10). The Holy Spirit is here to communicate to you who have become Christians, who have become containers for The Anointed One in the earth, that you are indeed made righteous by the indwelling of the Holy One. You are made righteous so that God can speak and act and love and give through you. "Now then we are ambassadors for Christ...For He has made the One who knew no sin to become sin for us so that we might be made the righteousness of God in Him" (II Cor. 5:20,21). The Holy Spirit is here to draw you into the one purpose of God.

"...Of judgment, because the prince of this world is judged" (John 16:11). The Holy Spirit is here to communicate that you are no longer judged and neither is your neighbor, family, co-worker, fellow Christian. The devil is judged and condemned. You are now part of the enforcement team to stop his illegal operations in the earth.

You are called to perfection. (Matthew 5:48) But you can't be perfect without the Perfect One making Himself one with you.

One of my favorite passages of promise is in Hosea. "And I will betroth you to me forever. Yes, I will betroth you to me in righteousness, and in judgment, and in lovingkindness, and in mercies. I will even betroth you to me in faithfulness and you shall know the Lord" (Hosea 2:19,20).

This passage defines a progression which will be culminated in Paul's declaration of our future recorded in Ephesians 5:27: "that He might present it to Himself a glorious church, not having spot, or wrinkle, or any such thing; but that it should be holy and without blemish."

God promised to make you one with Himself in righteousness. That was accomplished in Jesus Christ on the Cross and received as you acknowledge your need and desire for that righteousness, that right standing with God.

God promised to make you one with Himself in judgment, in mental processes, in verdicts about the way things are. That was accomplished as men received and recorded His Word and put it together so that you can input it and feed the New Creation man within and become one with His Truth, having the mind of Christ.

God promised to make you one with Himself in lovingkindness. That is the actions you do of kindness and generosity and mercy at His prompting.

God promised to make you one with Him in mercies. This is His own heart of compassion and mercy, not just His action but His emotion, experienced by you toward others. You are not called to feel something but to do something. He will provide the feelings after you provide the actions.

God promised to even betroth you unto Himself in <u>faithfulness</u>. Can you imagine being the same "yesterday, today, and forever" (Hebrews 13:8) like Jesus, not being tossed about with every mental wave of doctrine or emotional wave of desire?

God promised that you would know Him. This word "know" is the same word that was used of Adam when he "knew" his wife. It is a word of intimacy and perception. Paul said "...then I shall know, even as also I am known" (I Cor. 13:12). How wonderful will that be?

When you accepted Jesus Christ as your Savior, God began this process of transformation in you. From Righteousness of relationship when you were born again, to His Judgement in your mind (Romans 2:2) as you choose His Word, to Lovingkindness as you submit your will to obey His promptings of action and speech, to Mercies as He makes your very emotions one with His, to Faithfulness as He purifies you to His singleness of purpose, to Oneness with Himself, the purpose and complete joy for which you were created.

God loves you. He purposed from the beginning of Creation that you would be one with Him, in fellowship and in character. "He has chosen us in Him before the foundation of the world, that we should be holy and without blame before Him in love" (Ephesians 1:4).

When you choose to cooperate with God's purpose, then His kingdom comes on earth.

You cooperate by believing Him and looking at Him as revealed in the mirror of His Word. He has given "the light of the knowledge of the glory of God in the face of Jesus Christ" (II Cor. 4:6).

We sing the hymn "Turn Your Eyes Upon Jesus". We wear shirts and bracelets that ask "What Would Jesus Do?" This is part of the present day work of the Holy

Spirit to get us to look in the mirror because "we all...beholding as in a mirror the glory of the Lord are changed into the same image from glory to glory by the Spirit of the Lord" (II Cor. 3:18).

Hallelujah!

In the very first chapter we looked at three armies that come against God's people: our cultural situation, our genetic heritage, and the evil spirits who come along with those things in order to defeat us....the world, the flesh, and the devil.

Those armies are the enemies of purity. But as always, you win by looking to the One who alone can defeat them, and by praising Him for His mercy that is always available to you You can't perfect yourself, but God can. What you can do is choose holiness, choose to not be impure, choose unpollution. Choose Shalom – completeness and wholeness in every area. And look at Jesus.

He will do the rest.

THINGS TO REMEMBER

The Battle Against Impurity

1. God has one purpose for you - oneness with Himself.

2. The Holy Spirit is here to show the world that the only sin God is holding anyone accountable for is not trusting in and relying on Jesus Christ.

3. The Holy Spirit is here to show Christians that they are made righteous so that God can move through them.

4. The Holy Spirit is here to show the world that all judgment is against the devil and his followers.

5. The Holy Spirit is here to change you into the image of God.

Scripture Truths

"The Lord shall establish thee an holy people unto Himself..."
Deut. 28:9

"He has chosen us in Him before the foundation of the world, that we should be holy and without blame before Him in love."
Ephesians 1:4

"that He might present it to Himself a glorious church, not having spot, or wrinkle, or any such thing; but that it should be holy and without blemish." Ephesians 5:27

"And I will betroth you to me forever. Yes, I will betroth you to me in righteousness, and in judgment, and in

lovingkindness, and in mercies. I will even betroth you to me in faithfulness and you shall know the Lord." Hosea 2:19,20

BLESSED ARE THE PURE IN HEART FOR THEY SHALL SEE GOD. Matthew 5:8

Chapter Seventeen

The Battle Against Death

"For he must reign, till he has put all enemies under his feet. The last enemy that shall be destroyed is death."

I Corinthians 15:25,26

When I was a child I sat in church looking at the golden grillwork behind the choir and thinking about the stairs behind that grill, the golden stairway that led to heaven. I really wanted to go up those steps and be where there was always happiness and lots of ice cream. Looking back I wonder where I got that concept.

I thought it was virtuous of me to prefer heaven to earth. I realize now that I just wanted to escape. I wanted to leave my body behind and go where it could no longer trouble me with either pain or temptation. It was decades before I learned that God never wanted a separation of heaven and earth, of soul and body.

This insight began at the funeral of the mother of a friend of mine, an African American family. My daughter and I were the only Caucasians at the service and I remember thinking that these people knew how to show grief; they didn't act polite and reserved like all the funerals I had been to previously. They wept and wailed and showed that something awful had happened by the loss of their sister in the Lord.

It seemed to my mind that there was a lot of emotionalism but I could tell that the Holy Spirit was there in greatly felt Presence. Everyone filed past the coffin and when I did, I experienced a realization of perversion. I saw how wrong it was for the soul to be separated from the body. I remembered how God had intended Adam to live forever and how He is going to change our corruptible bodies into incorruptible ones.

It was the beginning for me of agreeing with God that death is an enemy to be overcome.

Yes, there are times that death comes as a relief from pain and therefore seems more like a friend than an enemy....but we must realize that pain was never intended by God either.

All sickness and dis-ease is incipient death, the physical symptom of physical separation from God. It is death working in the body, the enemy of Shalom, the enemy of the connectedness of spirit and flesh that Jesus came to restore.

The apostle Paul writes "Look, I show you a mystery; we shall not all sleep but we shall all be changed, in a moment in the twinkling of an eye, at the last trump; for the trumpet shall sound and the dead shall be raised incorruptible, and we shall be changed. For this corruptible must put on incorruption and this mortal must put on immortality.

So when this corruptible shall have put on incorruption, and this mortal shall have put on immortality, then shall be brought to pass the saying that is written Death is swallowed up in victory" (I Cor. 15:51 – 54).

In that last phrase, "Death is swallowed up in victory," Paul was quoting from Isaiah 25:8 where God also promises to make a feast for all people and "destroy the face of the covering cast over all people" (verse 7). I think that is interesting since the devil was originally the "anointed cherub that covers" (Ezekiel 28:14). The enemy of God, the accuser of the brethren, the father of lies, the prince of this world, the wrong covering cast over all people, will be destroyed and "the Lord God will wipe away tears from off all faces" (Isaiah 25:8).

The day will come when death will be no more and physical bodies will live forever; indeed the whole physical creation will be so inundated with the life of God that the universe will truly BE a uni-verse, spiritual and physical realms become one.

There are many schools of thought of when and how and in what order this restoration of all God is to all He has created will come. We are not going to try to answer that mystery here.

People love to discuss "end times."

Will the church be changed in a twinkling of an eye before the tribulation? Will the church be changed in a twinkling of an eye in the middle of the tribulation? Will it happen after the tribulation?

Is the tribulation period a real time frame or is it symbolic? Is there a real millennial reign of Jesus Christ as King in the earth or is that symbolic?

Does Jesus come back two different times, once for His Church and once to set up government...or is there just one Coming of Christ?

Premillennial, postmillenial, amillenial, pretribulation, midtribulation, posttribulation. I have my theories and you have yours and the rest of our brothers and sisters have theirs. But guess what? Our theories are not what is going to cause the Second Coming of the Lord Jesus Christ to happen. And when it does happen, it is not going to matter what we thought about it.

What does matter is that we long for His coming.

Paul wrote "...there is laid up for me a crown of righteousness which the Lord, the righteous judge, shall give me at that day: and not to me only, but unto all them also that love his appearing" (II Timothy 4:8).

The second coming of Christ is something the whole Church agrees will happen, though we may differ in what we believe about how and when. It is a right thing to love His appearing, to long for the day when we see Him face to face.

Why? Not because of a childish desire like I had, to escape the problems of this world, but because that longing for His coming is a symptom of the heart that belongs to Him.

As I told a lady once who had been taught to fear the appearing of the Lord Jesus Christ, "It's like having a pen pal that you grow to love. You start by writing letters back and forth (prayer and Bible reading); then you begin talking on the phone (meditation and prayer and listening to the Holy Spirit); and then you find out you are going to meet in person and you can hardly wait."

Once during the four years that I held services at a campground from April to November, there was a group there from a Seminary who had come apart for the weekend to seek the Lord. That was the largest group we had ever had at a campground service – in the thirties instead of our usual five to twelve. I asked the question "How many people think that the rapture of the church may happen in your lifetime?" Every hand there went up.

I was stunned by the realization that not one of us present believed in our own death.

I remembered that John wrote, "this is the victory that overcomes the world, even our faith" (I John 5:4). When enough of the Body of Christ does not believe in their own death but believes in the eternal life being manifested in our bodies, will it make a difference?

I think so.

The word rapture comes from the Latin "Raptura" a translation of the Greek word "harpazo" which means to seize and catch up. It is translated "caught up" in English in II Thessalonians 4:17 "Then we which are alive and remain shall be caught up together with them in the clouds to meet the Lord in the air: and so shall we ever be with the Lord."

No matter what we call this event when we are physically united with the Lord, it is an exciting time and also referred to as "that blessed hope, and the glorious appearing of the great God and our Savior Jesus Christ" (Titus 2:13).

We know that we are not supposed to speculate on when Jesus is coming again with restoration (Acts 1:7) but we are supposed to be aware of the signs of the times when He will come (Matthew 24:32-35).

Israel is a nation again for the first time in nearly 2,000 years. Much of the prophecy concerning the second coming could not happen until Israel was established as a nation.

Jesus promised to present His Church "to himself a glorious church, not having spot, or wrinkle, or any such thing; but that it should be holy and without blemish" (Ephesians 5:27). Peter says that we are to be the type of persons who have "holy conversation and godliness, looking for and hastening the coming of the day of God" (II Peter 3:11,12).

Some people say, "Keep your eyes on Israel" to know when and how God is moving toward this event. Some people say, "Keep your eyes on the Church". I think both are true.

You can do nothing about God's prophecies concerning Israel, except pray, but you will hasten the day of the Lord by your submission to His process of sanctification, cleansing you, and filling you with His character.

And it could be that the Old Jerusalem and the New Jerusalem are intertwined in ways we do not understand yet. (Hebrews 12:22; Psalm 122:6)

"...the marriage of the Lamb is come, and his wife has made herself ready...Blessed are they which are called to the marriage supper of the Lamb.." (Revelation 19:7-9).

The Lamb of God is Jesus who gave His life to purchase a Bride. Just as the first Adam was put to sleep and God took something from His side and built him a wife, so Jesus was put to the sleep of death, and blood and water poured from His side with which the Father is building Him a wife. You are a member of that Bride of Christ who will live forever with His eternal life.

THERE IS NO SIN TOO BIG TO KEEP HIM FROM LOVING YOU! THERE IS NO SIN SMALL ENOUGH TO TAKE WITH YOU TO THE MARRIAGE SUPPER OF THE LAMB.

The Marriage Supper of the Lamb is the time when you will be made completely one with the Spirit of Christ, your entire mind, emotions, will, and body one with Him.

We are the Body of Christ, the Vessel of the Anointed One. He needs every one of us here in the physical realm so He can speak, love, give, heal, teach, and forgive through us.

You are no longer God's creation, but His child. When Jesus was first born into the earth, He was called the "only begotten Son" of God (John 3:16) but after the death and resurrection of the only begotten son, He is called "the firstbegotten" (Hebrews 1:6) and "the firstborn from the dead" (Colossians 1:18) and "the firstborn among many brothers" (Romans 8:29).

You are now a son/daughter/child of God, if you have been born again by inviting the life of Jesus Christ in to your heart; you are now begotten not created. And you are to "work out your own salvation with fear and trembling for it is God which works in you both to will and do of his good pleasure" (Philippians 2:12,13). You are re-born of the Eternal Spirit, never to die.

Hebrews 2:14 and 15 tells us "Forasmuch as the children are partakers of flesh and blood, he also himself likewise took part of the same that through death he might destroy him who had the power of death, that is the devil, and deliver them who through fear of death were all their lifetime subject to bondage." I want us to look carefully at what that means.

Strong's Concordance defines the Greek word thanatos, translated death in this passage, as "death, has the basic meaning of separation of 1) the soul from the body...2) man from God...Adam died on the day he disobeyed God and hence all mankind are born in the same spiritual condition."

Think about that. You were born dead...born with a soul separated from God, born into the darkness of separation from God physically, morally, and intellectually, the exact opposite of light. That is the Strong's Concordance definition of the darkness mentioned in Col. 1:3 and I Peter 2:9. You have been delivered from the authority of physical, moral, and intellectual darkness and into the Kingdom of God's dear Son (Col. 1:3). You have been called out of physical, moral, and intellectual darkness into His marvelous light (I Peter 2:9)!

Jesus said, "Whosoever lives and believes in me shall never die" (John 11:26).

Jesus said that two millennia ago. Since many who called themselves Christians have died physically, does that mean no one has ever believed in Him? No, it means that dead souls who chose life, those who have chosen oneness with, instead of separation from, God and who trust in and rely on Jesus, will never be separated from Him again. We also have a promise that eventually the entire physical realm will be reconnected with Him and all those who live in Him. (Romans 8: 21 – 23)

I believe that time is coming soon.

In the spring of 1968 I woke up very alert at 3:30 a.m. and felt the Holy Spirit calling me outside. I went out and looked up at the stars and thought how much history had passed on the earth under that same sky. I thought about the pre-civil war period in America that had always appealed to me, and sixteenth century England that had always interested me, and Egypt under the Pharaohs that had fascinated me as a child. And then I heard the voice of the Holy Spirit, "You are living in the most exciting time in the history of the world." I didn't think so because my life at the time was a little boring. I thought surely the time Jesus walked in the earth was the most exciting time in the history of the world from God's point of view, but since I knew it was the Spirit of God speaking, I didn't argue but remained silent. After a few minutes I went back into the house and back to bed.

The next night the same thing happened. I woke up promptly at 3:30 a.m., went out in the yard, looked up at the sky and thought about the history of the world and heard "You are living in the most exciting time in the history of the world."

The third night in a row the exact same thing happened. I awoke at 3:30 a.m., went out in the yard, looked up at the sky, thought about the history of the world and heard "You are living in the most exciting time in the history of the world." Only this time, the Holy Spirit went on to say more.

"There is a time of separation coming. The forces are gathering. Light is getting lighter and dark is getting darker." And I saw what appeared to be a gray mass and it began to separate into light and dark. I knew that grayness represented the generation that was passing away, the confusion about who God is and what He does and who the Church is; it represented apathy and ignorance.

That was in 1968 and what a separation we have seen!

Sin of all kinds which originally evoked horror are now accepted and legalized or in the process of being legalized. Murder, abuse, and every kind of evil is in our land in epidemic proportions. Christianity which was for decades taken for granted in the USA is now disdained and expressions of it made illegal in places.

And yet, Concerts of Prayer, ecumenical gatherings of all types, Christian bumper stickers, billboards and teeshirts, the Word of God on the airwaves – TV, Radio, tapes, CD's, Internet - also abound.

And if you haven't been separated from some of the behavior of the "old man", you will be soon. "Yet once more I shake not the earth only, but also heaven. And this word, 'yet once more' signifies the removing of those things that are shaken, as of things that are made, so that those things which cannot be shaken may remain. Therefore since we are receiving a kingdom which cannot be moved, let us have grace so that by grace we may serve God acceptably with reverence and godly fear. For our God is a consuming fire" (Hebrews 12:26 – 29).

You are loved and God intends to make you perfect. He intends to make you perfect spirit, soul, and body.

He is working in you to flood your heart, mind, and will with His character and nature, to make your soul one with Himself. And when that oneness has completely happened, your body will be flooded with the Life too.

Death of every kind will have been defeated.

And the Life God intended for you in the beginning can begin.

THINGS TO REMEMBER

The Battle Against Death

1. God created mankind a soul in a body to live forever by His Life, His Spirit, flowing through them.

2. God has now begotten a new race, born of His Spirit and character, to live forever in a body.

3. God wants you to eagerly look forward to the time when Jesus comes and you are changed to be like Him in every way.

4. Fight death by believing in eternal life flooding the physical realm.

Scripture Truths

"For he must reign, till he has put all enemies under his feet. The last enemy that shall be destroyed is death."

I Corinthians 15:25,26

"We shall not all sleep but we shall all be changed...So when this corruptible shall have put on incorruption, and this mortal shall have put on immortality, then shall be brought to pass the saying that is written Death is swallowed up in victory."

I Corinthians 15:51,54

IF THE SPIRIT OF HIM THAT RAISED UP JESUS FROM THE DEAD DWELLS IN YOU, HE THAT RAISED UP CHRIST FROM THE DEAD SHALL ALSO QUICKEN YOUR MORTAL BODIES. Romans 8:11

AND THE VERY GOD OF PEACE SANCTIFY YOU WHOLLY; AND I PRAY YOUR WHOLE SPIRIT AND SOUL AND BODY BE PRESERVED BLAMELESS UNTO THE COMING OF OUR LORD JESUS CHRIST.
I Thess. 5:23

APPENDIX

This section gives two applications for each chapter in the book: "How To Pray" and "Study Questions."

Before publication, these applications were used by several groups during 17 week studies in which those involved read the chapters and then prayed and discussed together. The material has also been successfully used by individuals. The "How To Pray" section is before the "Study Questions" for those who want to pray but are not ready to go in depth with the questions at that time.

Be sure and go back and read the "Things To Remember" page with all the scripture verses before study or prayer for that chapter.

The "How To Pray" suggestions will work best for you if you read every scripture that is referenced before you pray. And take the time to really pray with your mind and heart. Communicate with the Lord as if He were right there with you. In truth, He is! *"I am with you always, even to the end of the world"* (Matthew 28:20.)

The "Study Questions" will be most effective if you take the time to think them through and let the Lord show you what is in your mind and heart. He already knows! And again, if there is a scripture reference, stop and read it.

If there are things you don't feel comfortable answering in a group, wait until you are alone before searching your heart and mind concerning them...but don't skip over them if you want to be free! It is very helpful to have at least one friend to share with so they can agree with you in prayer and encourage you in your journey to victory.

My prayer for you is that you receive all that Jesus died to give you and become a victorious warrior in Him and for Him, increasing the Kingdom on earth, as it is in heaven.

SHALOM!

CHAPTER ONE

HOW TO PRAY

God gave us His Word for the purpose of having us agree with it in our desires and actions. When we put His Word in our mouths, agreeing with His thoughts poured forth, that Word will come to pass. **"My Word shall not return to me void, but it shall accomplish that which I please, and it shall prosper in the thing whereto I sent it" (Isaiah 55:11).**

The first principle of spiritual warfare is ONLY GOD CAN DEFEAT EVIL; therefore your first prayer must be one of surrender to God's power. Jehoshaphat prayed "We have no might...but our eyes are upon thee" (II Chronicles 20:12). Your own praying about any situation must begin with a realization of your helplessness.

It must continue with a realization of His desire to help you. "He who comes to God must believe that He IS and that He is a rewarder of them that diligently seek Him" (Hebrews 11:6).

If you believe that He wants to be powerful in your situation then it becomes easy to praise Him for what He is doing and will do for you. And your sincere praise is a spiritual weapon that will drive the enemy away from that situation.

STUDY QUESTIONS

1. What areas have you thought you needed to help God with before He can successfully defeat evil in your life?
    Ex: reputation, health, finances, habits, relationships, career success, ministry, education.

2. What does it mean to you to praise God? Have you ever praised Him with vain repetitions?

3. What things in your genetic makeup or inherited patterns of behavior can you see are enemies of your perfect happiness, health, and success?

4. What things in our present society have you "bought into" that do not match up with what the Bible says about truth?

5. Can you see areas in your life where the forces of evil have used those things to kill, steal, and destroy what God wants for you?

6. How can words change things?

CHAPTER TWO

HOW TO PRAY

Acknowledge that like the man in the story recorded in Mark 9:17-27, you believe but your belief is mixed with unbelief; you have faith but it is mixed with doubt and fear.

Admit that you, like Job's friends, have spoken wrongly about God (Job 42:7) and that like Job himself, you have often spoken of things that you didn't understand (Job 42:3).

Confess that your words have often been "stout against" God (Malachi3:13). Ask Him to forgive you for every idle word you have ever spoken (Matt. 12:36,37).

Cry out to Him, "Set a watch, O Lord, before my mouth; keep the door of my lips" (Psalm 141:3). And ask Him that the words of your mouth and the meditation of your heart will be acceptable in His sight (Psalm 19:14).

God desires that you understand Him and His mercy. (Hosea 6:6)

Give Him permission to wash away any wrong thoughts or ideas you have about Him and replace them with Truth about who He is and what He wants for you.

STUDY QUESTIONS

1. What have you believed about the sovereignty of God in relation to what happens in the world?

2. What part do you think faith plays in what happens in the world?

3. Does this principle – WHAT YOU BELIEVE AND SPEAK ABOUT GOD'S CHARACTER AND WILL DETERMINES WHAT HE CAN DO FOR

YOU – cause any confusion to you? Does it war with your world view?

4. Have you ever attributed something to God that you would think badly of one human being for doing to another human being?

5. Do you believe that your words have any power?

6. What do you think about this statement…GOD HAS INVESTED HIS SOVEREIGNTY OVER THE WORLD IN HIS WORD THROUGH THE FAITH OF HIS PEOPLE.

CHAPTER THREE

HOW TO PRAY

Confess that you, like the Galatians, have tried to reach perfection by your own works (Galatians 3:3). Confess that you have not believed that Jesus paid the price for all your sins to the extent of redeeming you from the bad things that happen because you have not fully obeyed the law. Confess that you have believed that you need to pay the price for some of the sins you have committed.

Ask God for a revelation of His power to you (Ephesians 1:17-23).

Ask God to help you remember to stay 'hid in Him' (Colossians 3:3) and to intentionally put on the 'armor of God' so that you may stand against the schemes of the devil against your life and God's purpose for you (Ephesians 6:13).

STUDY QUESTIONS

1. What does the term "curse of the law" mean to you?

2. What do you think the devil wants to happen to you in this world?

3. What do you honestly believe that God wants your time in this world to be like?

4. What is a blessing?

5. What does "put on the armor of God" mean to you?

6. Review the seven principles of spiritual warfare. Which one(s) do you have trouble believing?

1. Only God can successfully defeat evil.
2. Praise of God brings God on the scene.
3. Evil attacks on three fronts.
4. What you believe about God's character and will determines what He can do for you.
5. God only wants good things for you.
6. Christians are redeemed from the bad things that happen as a result of not obeying God's law.
7. Your armor and weaponry are the Word of God.

CHAPTER FOUR

HOW TO PRAY

Ask the Lord to make you a part of the answer instead of being a part of the problem. Ask Him for a greater revelations of Peace: Shalom – wholeness, completeness, and connectedness.

Ask God to let you see things in this world as He sees them. Daily, seek His perception and His will concerning the state of your soul and the circumstances around you.

Pray "Thy Kingdom come, Thy will be done on earth as it is in heaven" (Matt. 6:10) knowing that you are setting yourself in agreement with God's original plan of the spiritual and physical worlds being completely connected through mankind (Genesis 1:26-28).

STUDY QUESTIONS

1.   a. What has the word "Peace" meant to you before you received the information in this chapter?

    b. Do you have a different concept of peace now?

2. What occasions have brought pure joy to you?

3. Can you sometimes differentiate between your will, your mind, and your heart in a situation?

4. Have you ever been aware of Chaos – situations and circumstances that you knew at the time were separated from God and His will?

5. Does it help you at all to think of individual battles against things like sickness, shame,

depression, poverty, anxiety, and shame as part of a war?

6. Can you see that every victory you win in small battles helps establish God's peace over the chaos of the enemy in the earth?

CHAPTER FIVE

HOW TO PRAY

Ask the Lord to show you 1. the things in your heart for which you have never received His forgiveness 2. the things for which you have never forgiven yourself. Confess that it is pride to think that your sinfulness is beyond the Blood of Jesus to wash away.

Read I John 1:9 and repeat it out loud, making it personal, **"If I confess my sin, the Lord is faithful and just to forgive my sin and to cleanse me of all unrighteousness."** Confess your sin and agree that the punishment for it was taken by Jesus on the Cross; tell Him that you receive His Blood cleansing you from the sinfulness in your nature that was the cause of that sinful act. Thank Him for forgiving you and ask Him to help you forgive yourself.

Ask the Lord to reveal to you the unforgiveness that you have held against others. Tell Him that you forgive_____ for what they did to you and that you consider their wrong actions paid for by Him. Ask Him to forgive them too. Ask Him to pull any bitterness and hatred from your heart. Thank Him that He has forgiven them and will keep you walking in forgiveness toward them.

STUDY QUESTIONS

1. What is forgiveness?

2. Is there anyone you have not forgiven...anyone you think should pay for what they have done to you or someone else?

3. Do you think it is right for someone to go free from repercussions when they have done something wrong?

4. Do you ever recognize your own faults in the people who make you the most irritated?

5. Have you forgiven yourself for all your sins and failures and weaknesses?

6. Do you really believe that your forgiveness of others and self makes a difference in life? Whose life?

7. Do you believe that your forgiveness from God is dependent on your forgiveness of others?

CHAPTER SIX

HOW TO PRAY

Be honest with yourself and God. Don't ever pretend to yourself or Him that you are happy if you are not. Confess that you know, even if you don't feel, that He has a good future planned for you. Confess that your sorrow or despair is less than His Plan for you and you know that. Thank Him for understanding the state of your heart. Receive His love and forgiveness for your human weakness. Ask Him to show you if you have a chemical imbalance or other physical problem. If you think He is leading you to seek medical help, do it!!!

Read Isaiah 61:3. Ask Him to give you strength to praise Him even though you don't feel like it. Let Him show you Himself taking the spirit of heaviness and throwing it out the door. Let Him show you Himself placing a garment of praise around your shoulders. Put on some praise and worship cd's and let the music draw you into worshipping Him. Tell Him that you give your future into His hands, and will trust Him with all the days of your life. Each day, recommit that day to Him.

STUDY QUESTIONS

1. Can you remember a time when you felt overwhelmed 'crushed and overpowered, poured down on and buried beneath' about something?

2. When you have felt overwhelmed, did you look to other people to relieve the pressure, or did you look to God?

3. Does the world seem more powerful to you than the power of God and the blood of Jesus?

4. What does this mean to you? "Joy is all about triumph and victory in life. Depression is all about hopelessness and failure in life." Do you believe it? Have you ever felt guilty for being depressed?

5. What does it mean to you to be redeemed from the curse of the law?

CHAPTER SEVEN

HOW TO PRAY

Admit to yourself and to God that anxiety comes from not trusting Him completely. Forgive yourself and ask Him to forgive you for imperfect faith in Him.

Ask Him to show you if you need medical help and if so, get it!

Ask Him to show you any steps you need to take in any situation that needs resolving. If nothing comes to mind, then trust that He is working it out without your help. If something comes to mind, ask Him to let you know if it is your own thought or guidance from Him. Trust that He will do so.

See yourself taking the situation that causes you anxiety and putting it in a box and taking that box to the throne of God. Leave it there with Him.

Thank Him that He cares about every tiny circumstance of your life and that you can trust Him to handle all the things that concern you.

STUDY QUESTIONS

1. Have you ever been in a situation that tested your faith in God's love for you and His promises to help you?

2. Do you believe, really believe deep down in your heart, that you can trust God to give you a good future? Do you think you deserve a bad future?

3. Have you ever thought it humility to refuse to trust in your own abilities, resources, or goodness and to trust in God for everything?

4. Have you ever thought that to not believe in something the Bible promises is to call God a liar?

5. Have you ever been able to completely cast the care of something over on God without taking it back? If so, how did He resolve it?

6. Can you make a decision to start trusting God because **"God has not given you a spirit of fear, and His Perfect Love casts out fear?"** (II Timothy 1:7; I John 4:18)

CHAPTER EIGHT

HOW TO PRAY

Thank God that He can see an overall picture of your life, even though your vision is very limited. Thank Him that He has the perfect wisdom for you concerning every situation. Thank Him that He cares for you beyond your understanding.

Read James 1:5-8 aloud. Then personalize it, "Lord, I lack wisdom in this situation and I am asking you to give me wisdom. I am asking with faith in You and Your desire to guide me. I will not waver and will trust that Your wisdom will come to me."

Tell Him that you trust Him to lead you with His peace and assurance. Thank Him for His wisdom and guidance.

STUDY QUESTIONS

1. Can you think of times in the past when you have been confused, when you have had "two minds" -or more- about a situation?

2. Have any of those times been resolved and you could see how a deception was placed in your mind or emotions by the devil?

3. Have you ever identified wrong motives in yourself that aided in your confusion and lack of desire to truly hear God's will?

4. Is there a situation in your life right now where you are confused?

5. Can you identify different voices in that confusion?

6. Can you sort out those voices in the present or past by scripture and knowledge of your own weaknesses?

CHAPTER NINE

HOW TO PRAY

Thank God for His Life at work inside you that allows you to pray as Jesus prays. Ask Him to give you a revelation of the devil as your enemy and of other human beings as special individuals for whom Jesus died and the Father views as important.

"Father, I hold up _____ to you. I thank you for their life because they are a child of yours for whom Jesus died. I ask you to bless them, win them to your truth and love, and deliver them from the power of darkness into the kingdom of light. Lead me in any way that You want me to show Your love to them. In Jesus Name, Amen."

And then listen. And then obey!

STUDY QUESTIONS

1. Have you ever prayed for "**all** men?" (I Timothy 2:1)

2. Have you ever "cursed" anyone?

3. Have you ever blamed God for something that killed, stole, or destroyed? (John 10:10)

4. Have you ever "heaped coals of fire on someone" in God's way? (Romans 12:20)

5. Is there a situation right now in your life where you need to recognize the difference between the person and the true enemy?

CHAPTER TEN

HOW TO PRAY

Thank the Lord that He has made many promises to you about the future. Thank Him that He has sent His Word to you so that you can receive that Word and let it become flesh in your circumstances.

Find the promises of protection in Psalm 91 and other places in the Bible and read them out loud. Print them out and hang them in places that you see them often. Read them and make them personal.

"Thank you, Lord that you give Your angels guard over me to keep me in all my ways. Thank you that my heart can safely trust in You and Your protection." (Psalm 91)

STUDY QUESTIONS

1. Are you, or have you ever been, afraid of accidents happening to you or your loved ones:
    a. in certain circumstances
    b. in uncertain times of the future?

2. Does the concept of man being in authority in the earth seem frightening to you? Does it seem blasphemous to you?

3. Do you believe that God makes promises to mankind?

4. To you, is the Bible more like:

    a. A history book
    b. A "how to" manual

    c. A script

5. Discuss the differences in those three descriptions with a friend.

6. Can you think of any times that the Word of God has changed the natural course of things in your life?

7. Has this chapter helped your understanding of the sovereignty of God?

8. Do you disagree with this understanding of the sovereignty of God or do you think this will help you have a more accurate worldview?

CHAPTER ELEVEN

HOW TO PRAY

Ask God to rid your mind of any wrong thinking about Him and material things. Ask Him to give you a right picture of His desire to provide your needs.

Ask Him to show you times and ways that you have tried to be your own provider. When you see them, ask Him to forgive you for trusting in something other than Him.

Thank Him that He IS your Provider.

Hold up any need you have to Him and tell Him that you want to trust Him to provide that need for you. Ask Him to do it. And thank Him for providing it. Ask Him to remind you that He is now in charge of your receiving it.

Praise Him for being the perfect provider who never lacks anything and is able to take the smallest amount of anything and make it enough.

STUDY QUESTIONS

1. Have you ever had a time when you were deficient in material goods or money? If so, list them:

2. Have you ever been taught that poverty is a virtue?

3. Have you ever given to God out of necessity or grudgingly? (II Corinthians 9:7,8)

4. Do you believe that God wants to give you everything you desire? (Romans 8:31,32)

5. Have you ever had God provide something to you that was not a need but a luxury?

6. Have you ever been used by God to provide something to others? A need? A luxury?

CHAPTER TWELVE

HOW TO PRAY

Ask the Lord to show you if there is any reason hidden in your heart that makes you want to be sick (need rest, attention, freedom from responsibility, etc.) If there is, ask Him to show you how that hidden desire is against His will for you; let Him remind you that He can give you the things you need without sickness getting them for you. If there is something there, ask Him to forgive you for harboring it and ask Him to root it out and give you strength to get back into the war against Chaos.

When you are sure your own heart is not warring against God's promises for health, choose a healing scripture verse to receive – a Word to become flesh in your body. Read that verse out loud and make it personal (Example Psalm 103:3). "Thank you, Lord that you heal all my diseases. You are the Healer and I trust You to heal me. Give me wisdom to know what to do in this situation. Do I go to the doctor, take medicine, change habits, or just believe Your promise without any other action on my part?"

Trust Him to give you wisdom, knowing that it is His will that you be healed. He knows you better than you know yourself...and He knows how you can best receive the healing He offers.

STUDY QUESTIONS

1. Have you ever felt like God must have caused your sickness for some reason...Examples: you got more attention from others, you paid more attention to God; you learned something while you were sick;

you were unable to do something you shouldn't have done?

2. Have you ever thought about what it means for mankind to "know" both good and evil?

3. Are you always sure what is good – coming from God – and what is evil – coming from the devil or fallen nature?

4. Do you believe that God has set the Body of Christ against sickness and disease?

5. Have you ever prayed for someone to receive healing from a sickness or disease? Did your prayer make a difference?

6. Have you ever been healed miraculously? With medical help? Without medical help?

CHAPTER THIRTEEN

HOW TO PRAY

Give the Lord permission to show you His love for the person with whom you are not in harmony. Let the Lord show you how much He loves you. Remind yourself that Jesus died for that other person just as surely as He died for you.

Ask the Lord to show you your fault in the relational brokenness. Confess that fault and receive forgiveness. Ask Him to cause the other person to forgive you.

Ask the Lord to show you the fault of the other person in the relational brokenness. Forgive the person and ask God to forgive them.

Hold up the relationship to God and make Jesus Lord over it. Trust Him to work and restore harmony.

Pray any scriptures you know concerning your particular relationships, believing that they will "become flesh" in your circumstances.

STUDY QUESTIONS

1. Have you ever chosen a relationship with a person over a relationship with God?

2. Has anyone ever gotten angry with you because you chose a relationship with God over your relationship with them? Have you ever gotten angry with someone for choosing God over you?

3. Have you ever had the Sword of the Word separate you from a person or group?

4. Has divorce ever affected your life? In a good way or a bad way?

5. Have you ever used your Covenant with God to pray for your child or grandchild?

6. Have your rights ever been more important to you than your righteousness...and hindered you walking in grace toward others?

CHAPTER FOURTEEN

HOW TO PRAY

Ask the Lord to shine light in the areas of your heart where shame is hiding. Ask Him if there is any self hatred there. Whatever He shows you, hand it to Him and ask Him to replace it with His love and grace for you.

Ask Him to forgive you for any pride that makes you think you are morally superior to any other human. Ask Him to help you understand that you are in the same state as other humans, in need of His grace.

Thank Him for teaching you that all you receive from Him is because of Grace and Mercy. Receive being separated completely from both shame and pride.

Glory in your freedom to be loved by God, self, and others...just because you are you and God is Love!

STUDY QUESTIONS

1. Have you ever felt ashamed of yourself for something you did wrong?

2. Have you ever felt ashamed of yourself for something done to you by someone else, or something done by someone close to you?

3. Do you feel shame because of who you are: your personality, family background, lack of something in your life?

4. Does this progression make sense to you?

CAUSE>FEELING OF INADEQUACY>SHAME>FEAR

(Cause is an action by self or others)

5. Can you see how shame can be the result of pride?

6. Can you begin to relax and let God make you into what He wants you to be? Can you let Him be your righteousness?

CHAPTER FIFTEEN

HOW TO PRAY

Sit quietly before the Lord and ask Him to show you what or who you have put before Him...what or who you enjoy more than Him...what or who you spend more money or time on than Him...what or who you think about more than Him...what or who you are more obedient to than Him...what or who you depend on more than Him.

When you have recognized these things, hold them out to Him and recognize that they are idols. Be willing to love Him more and put Him first.

"Father, forgive me for putting these things (or people) before You. Please cleanse my heart of all idols. Teach me how to love you with all my heart and soul and strength and mind."

STUDY QUESTIONS

1. What do you think about when you are all by yourself?

2. Are there any unfulfilled visions in your life?

3. What things are really important to you in your life? (possessions, positions)

4. What people in your life would you have a hard time giving up?

5. What would you do if God asked you to give them up?

6. What do you bow down to? In other words, what or who is controlling your actions?

CHAPTER SIXTEEN

HOW TO PRAY

Ask the Lord if there are any impurities in your heart that are keeping you from seeing Him clearly.

Ask Him if there are things from which you are ready to let Him purify you. Hold up those things and be still before Him, letting Him show you all He wants to show you about the situation, whether it is a past or present action, an idol, a change He wants you to make, etc.

Tell Him that, despite your trembling heart, despite your fear of your own emotions, you trust Him.

Be still and let Him wash away all impurities with His Love for YOU!

Thank Him for making you one with Him in greater and greater measure.

STUDY QUESTIONS

1.
   a. Do you believe that God has a purpose for each person's life?
   b. Have you ever wondered about your purpose in life?
   c. Do you know your purpose in life?

2. Have you ever experienced being single-minded about something over a long period of time?

3. Have you ever experienced contrition – mourning over an inadequacy or weakness of your personality, not just an action you took?

4. Can you see a difference in the "Christ-like-ness" in your life now and your life 10 years ago? In what areas?

5. What does the word "holiness" mean to you?

6. What will you be like when you are transformed into His image, made perfectly conformed to His likeness and yet still you?

CHAPTER SEVENTEEN

HOW TO PRAY

Ask God to show you how He wants you to think about death. Ask Him to teach you how He sees death. Ask Him for a greater revelation of SHALOM – wholeness, completeness, connectedness.

Place yourself, your body, your soul, completely in His hands and ask Him to help you trust Him with your whole self and your future.

Tell Him that you want Shalom, and ask Him to drive out chaos of any kind in you. Ask Him to drive out death with His resurrection life.

"Lord, put Your thoughts in my mind, Your desires in my will, Your passions in my heart, and Your Life in my body. Come, Lord Jesus…in me!"

STUDY QUESTIONS

1. What is your vision of heaven?

2. Have you ever wanted to leave this world?

3. Do you have strong beliefs about the end times, how it will happen?

4. How would you word your belief about God's goal for mankind?

5. Do you really believe that your actions can hasten the second coming? (II Peter 3:11,12)